THE
PRISONER
HANDBOOK

THE PRISONER
HANDBOOK

STEVEN PAUL DAVIES

Foreword by Alex Cox

to #1 — the towhead !

Love,
#2 & trying harder

B⬕XTREE

First published 2002 by Boxtree
an imprint of Pan Macmillan Ltd
Pan Macmillan, 20 New Wharf Road, London N1 9RR
Basingstoke and Oxford
Associated companies throughout the world
www.panmacmillan.com

ISBN 0 7522 1968 5

9 8 7 6 5 4 3 2 1

A CIP catalogue record for this book is
available from the British Library.

Typeset by seagulls
Printed and bound by Mackays of Chatham plc, Chatham, Kent

CONTENTS

ACKNOWLEDGEMENTS

My profoundest thanks and admiration go to those who've helped keep *The Prisoner* alive over the years – in particular, Karen and Roger Langley, David Barrie, Max Hora, David Healey and Roger Goodman. I also owe a debt of gratitude to all those who kindly sat down and contributed their memories of working on the series – Alexis Kanner, Kenneth Griffith, Anton Rodgers, Mark Eden, Jane Merrow, Norma West, Jack Lowin, Tony Sloman and Ian Rakoff.

I would like to thank Kirk Jacobson, Jools Holland, Fay Woolven at One Fifteen, Alex Close, Simon West, Tor McLaren, Jason Thorpe, Emma Keenan, Rebecca Edwards and all at Sci-Fi and Universal Studios Networks.

Thanks also to Tony Gale at Pictorial Press; David Quinlan at *TVTimes*; Spike in LA; Robin Llywelyn in Portmeirion; Caroline Tomlinson and Graham Nearn at Caterham; Tony Murray and Phil Weaver; Stephen McKay; Iris Griffith; John Goward and Ethel Yeates who all came forward with some great rare *Prisoner* photographs.

In terms of editorial assistance, I am indebted to Siobhan Gooley, Katy Carrington and Gordon Scott Wise at Macmillan, who made this book possible. And, as always, special thanks to Alex Cox and Tod Davies.

A MESSAGE FROM
SIX
OF
ONE
THE PRISONER APPRECIATION SOCIETY

The Prisoner Handbook is fully endorsed by Six of One, the *Prisoner* appreciation society.

In assisting with information and illustrations for Steven Paul Davies's excellent book, we have stood back to take a look at the achievements of *The Prisoner*'s official appreciation society so far. For a quarter of a century, *The Prisoner* and Six of One have been synonymous. The series has helped raise the profile of the society and in turn the society has brought world-wide attention to this television classic. Now that the series has appeared all round the globe and has been released on several different visual and audio formats, *The Prisoner* is one of the best-known TV works of all time.

We are pleased to have one of the society's members producing such a literate study of the programme and the people who are its loyal fans. The writer has already interviewed actors from the series, has had articles and press reports published and has supported Six of One over quite a few years. To him we are grateful and we hope that readers of his book will gain a clear insight into how *The Prisoner* came into being, how its own club was formed, and how both have endured. Six of One, whose Honorary President has been Patrick McGoohan throughout the existence of the society, is pleased to give its endorsement to Steven Paul Davies's research, revelations and reading material.

The society acknowledges that this is an independent handbook, rather than an 'official *Prisoner* guide'. The series and its themes have been explored in various ways and it is important that *The Prisoner* lives on in print through works such as Steven Paul Davies' *Handbook*.

Be seeing you,
Roger and Karen Langley,
Co-ordinators of Six of One

Six of One
Box 66,
Ipswich IP2 9TZ

FOREWORD

I saw *The Prisoner* when it was first shown on British TV. It is redundant to go on about how original it was, because there was nothing like it, before, or after. Kafka's name was bandied about later in connection with the series, and there are certainly overtones of Franz. But Kafkaesque is only one description of *The Prisoner*, valid if we assume that Number 6 is unconsciously a willing prisoner of the Village.

I suppose one can make the case for this. *The Prisoner*, like any artwork of genius, can be interpreted in diametrically opposing ways.

My take is that *The Prisoner* is not Kafkaesque at all. I didn't, as a teenager, watch it every week because the hero was a hopeless man like Joseph K. I watched it because I enjoyed – and empathized with – his predicament, and in the hope that he'd escape. For me, things in *The Prisoner* are, bizarrely, just as they appear. Number 6 is a real prisoner, coolly and determinedly wanting freedom, who – under cover of the blazer and detached air – thinks of nothing but escape.

Since the beginning of the Cold War the United States and the Soviet Union, Britain, China, France, and many other states, have subjected thousands of people to psychological torture in the name of 'national security'. These mental tortures are designed primarily to make the sufferers reveal information, and secondly to actually change their minds. Just as there really were sensory deprivation headphones, electric shock treatments and the MK-Ultra project, there must have been places like The Village: hermetically controlled artificial environments, where state-sponsored hostile debriefings or byzantine drug experiments could occur.

Number 6 is their prisoner. You could call him a victim. Yet he never accepts that he is either thing. Each week, on ITV, that cheesy commercial British TV channel, he struggled against some new weird trip laid on him by his captors, or he made an old-fashioned attempt to escape. His resistance was constant. He could be drugged, or physically beaten, and thrown back into his cottage, but he would not be bowed.

In this book, Steven Paul Davies makes an important point: McGoohan, in creating the series and the character, made Number 6 a non-violent character. His previous episodic TV character, John Drake in *Danger Man*, had been a hand-to-hand fighter who eschewed guns. This time McGoohan created a both passive, and pacifist, character. Davies suggests the creator of *The Prisoner* opposed violence on both ethical and religious grounds.

But passive protagonists are also those of great literature (*Absolom*, *Alice in Wonderland*, *Moby Dick*) and – strangely enough – great films (*Citizen Kane*, 2001, *Apocalypse Now*). Sometimes the series got so strange that Number 6 was a bemused witness, unable to understand or influence an insane scenario, only able to point the blazer and plot his escape.

I cannot remember an episode in which Number 6 was more than momentarily violent, and then in his own defence. This is not to say that *The Prisoner* itself wasn't shocking, or violent. There was the particularly bloodthirsty episode 'Living In Harmony' in which Number 6 was drugged and made to imagine himself a gunfighter in the Old West. Said gunfighter, like Gregory Peck in the eponymous film, refuses to return to his former ways, or to wear a badge. The violence of the episode was particularly anarchic and dragged-out, like that of a spaghetti Western. But Cowboy 6 would have none of it – instead, like Brando in *One Eyed Jacks* or Eastwood in *A Fistful of Dollars* opting to get endlessly beaten up.

The episode ended with his antagonists in the Western town reduced to cardboard cut-outs standing in the street. It was a great, unusual, unsettling hour of television. It was, probably for those reasons, the episode that wasn't broadcast when *The Prisoner* was later shown in the USA.

Because of the series' essential pacifism and surrealism, it isn't possible to eagerly await a big-budget Hollywood dose of soma called *The Prisoner*. The movie of *The Prisoner* is almost guaranteed to be another midatlantic blockbuster from the ITC back catalogue, by the team that brought you other hit movies where lots of things blow up.

The original *Prisoner* is a unique kettle of fish. McGoohan's series was brilliant because it was subtle, and surprising, and because of the charisma of its wry, non-violent, anti-authoritarian hero, who never gave up the struggle, who never gave up hope. McGoohan was that character. He conceived *The Prisoner*, and even wrote and directed some episodes.

The only *Prisoner* film that I will ever see is one directed by its creator, Patrick McGoohan!

Alex Cox
LIVERPOOL, MARCH 2002

INTRODUCTION

Have you ever wondered what it would be like
to live in a world of complete mistrust, having to
question everyone and everything? Well, in the
world you're about to experience, it becomes a
complete game – a game of survival.

'I am not a number I am a free man!': the words spoken by
Number 6 in every episode of *The Prisoner*. These words are
the essence of a television series which baffled a generation
and continues to intrigue a new one. But why write a book
to celebrate a 1960s television series? There are many worth-
while reasons.

The Prisoner is a television phenomenon and both the
production and the fan culture surrounding the series
deserve to be analysed. *The Prisoner Handbook* attempts to
examine the significance of the series now. Why is it still so
popular? Why does it have such a strong cult following?
What does it say about television audiences today? This
book is a complete study of the series as a whole, from its
conception, through the background struggles and personality clashes during production, to the huge world-wide
following that continues to grow.

INTRODUCTION

It doesn't take long to realize that beneath what is at one level a brilliant adventure series, there is something else – something much deeper. It becomes clear that Patrick McGoohan, who created the series as well as playing the title role, wanted to get across his own ideas about the society in which we live. He managed to do this in seventeen episodes of a complex, intelligent television series and succeeded in creating what has become one of the most talked-about television series of all time. This strange piece of television history deserves another look because even now, after more than thirty years, there are still many, many fans who 'want information'.

The Prisoner is manic fantasy but also symbolic of what is real: the struggle to remain an individual in a society increasingly obsessed with order and conformity. It encourages people to question and to think. When it first aired, each week twelve million viewers tuned in to this allegorical conundrum, an intelligent satire which provides a great commentary on our age. The whole series was clever, conniving and infuriating, with no answer to the big question: 'Why was he a prisoner?'

In America and Canada, the series has been used at degree level as a model for educational and sociological study. The Ontario Educational Communications Authority claimed that the series posed 'some of the crucial questions in the survival game humanity is playing; and it poses them in almost flawless film art. Like all great art, *The Prisoner* operates on many levels, the viewer gets as much or as little out of it as he chooses.' *The Prisoner* was drama to be taken seriously. Perhaps it has yet to be fully understood.

Today most programmes which claim to be innovative are still conservative enough to be given funding. *The Prisoner* really was something unusual; it was, and still is, *radical* – a true work of art which deserves our recognition. Now, more than thirty years on, it is a pleasure to take a fresh look and celebrate this classic TV series.

And how about *your* world?
Is it too late to wonder,
too late to cry?
Too late for a number
who never asked WHY?

Steven Paul Davies

CHAPTER ONE
ONE CRAZY IDEA

'It's so crazy, it just might work.'

– Lew Grade, 1966

'I can't conceive of anybody else in the world, then or now, giving me that amount of freedom with a subject which, in many respects, I suppose you might say was outrageous.'

– Patrick McGoohan on Lew Grade

With the launch of ITV on 22 September 1955, the BBC's twenty-year monopoly of British broadcasting came to an end. Commercial television brought an alternative to stuffy public service programming, and when Lew Grade formed a production company called ITC his instinct for business and his eye for talent resulted in stylish new programmes such as *The Adventures of Robin Hood*, *The Buccaneers* and *Emergency Ward Ten*, all hugely popular with the public and commercially successful. The big-budget series were feel-good fun. It was another of Grade's populist projects, the long-running 1960s television spy series *Danger Man*, that brought Patrick McGoohan international fame.

Danger Man was created by an Australian writer called Ralph Smart, and backed by Lew Grade. He targeted it at the overseas market, particularly the American television audience. It was one of the first spy series to appear on television and even beat Bond on to the screen (*Dr. No* wasn't released until 1961). The first episode was broadcast on 11 September 1960. The following year, it was screened with great success in America by the CBS network, as *Secret Agent*.

However, it wasn't an instant hit in the States and was revamped before further episodes – now hour-long shows – were seen. The story editor was George Markstein and Don Chaffey directed several episodes.

The character of John Drake was, like Number 6, a moral hero. Unlike the Bond-style spy, he never used a weapon and never got involved with a woman. Interviewed for a children's annual *The Television Star Book* in 1964, McGoohan talked honestly about how he made the producers change the character of John Drake:

> I didn't like the way the man came over when I started to read the scripts. He was painted as a rough, tough, sexy guy, who hit below the belt in his fights, was always using a gun, and making passes at pretty girls. I didn't like this conception of Drake. I wanted to change him, and I had a fight in getting my own way, but other people saw Drake as I did and so the change was made. Personally I hate violence. If Drake fights, then he has to fight clean. He will only use a gun in a desperate situation. And as for women – well, I don't want Drake to get too involved. He was a man who had to have complete freedom – freedom from any domestic situations.

McGoohan also has some strong words about the nature of interviews:

> I'm against any kind of invasion of my privacy. Most people want to talk about one's own personal and private life. They want to strip you of all your little secrets – find out the real you, as they say. Well, I understand they have a job to do, but I don't see why I should fall 'victim' to their inquisitive questions when they don't relate to my professional work. Anyone who wants to talk about me as an actor I'm only too happy to oblige.

Born in New York on 19th March 1928, Patrick McGoohan spent his childhood on his parents' Irish farm after they had left the United States. He later moved to Sheffield, where he spent some time in local amateur theatre. It was at the Sheffield Repertory Theatre, where he took a job as stage manager, that he met his wife, actress Joan Drummond.

It wasn't long before McGoohan became a major star in the theatre, where his early West End roles included an appearance in Orson Welles' adaptation of *Moby Dick*. He then played supporting parts in films such as *Passage Home* and *The Dam Busters* before signing a contract with the Rank Organisation in 1957 to appear in *Hell Drivers*, *High Tide at Noon*, *The Gypsy and the Gentleman* and *Nor the Moon by Night*.

In 1959, McGoohan was named Best Television Actor of the year for his roles in television plays such as *Brand* and *The Big Knife*. However, he achieved international celebrity status as John Drake in *Danger Man*.

It was in 1966, after he had tired of *Danger Man*, that he moved on to *The Prisoner*, the bizarre but brilliant piece of television filmed on location in the beautiful village of Portmeirion in North Wales.

Inevitably, comparisons between *Danger Man* and *The Prisoner* have been made. Although it was a 'classic' television series, with high production values compared to others of the time, *Danger Man* has never had as fanatical a following as *The Prisoner*. This is down to the fact that, although *Danger Man* was an intelligent series, it never had the consistent enigmatic slant of *The Prisoner*. *Danger Man* episodes which are fondly

EVERYMAN FILMS

M-G-M Studios,
Boreham Wood,
Herts, England.

Thank you for your generous letter; I am
grateful for a good run of the show and value
the support of our many followers.

Currently, I am engaged in preparation for a
new Series entitled " THE PRISONER " which
we hope will be with you some time in September
'67. If you care for prior information on this
please write me at the above address and I shall
be delighted to oblige.

Kind regards,

Cordially,

Patrick McGoohan

Patrick McGoohan

remembered (usually by fans of *The Prisoner*) tend to be those which *do* have that extra enigmatic edge to them. For example, many cite the 'Colony Three' episode, directed by Don Chaffey, as the one which actually inspired *The Prisoner*.

Many have stated that they believe the later character Number 6 was simply John Drake – they were both spies and both looked the same! However, McGoohan has always refuted such stories.

Whatever the truth is, it simply doesn't matter anyway. Each series has its own style and format. *The Prisoner* needs to be anonymous in order to form a vital part of the television allegory. He is an Everyman figure, created to appeal to everyone's desire for individuality. It doesn't matter that he was once a spy. It shouldn't matter that he may be called John Drake.

The very existence of *The Prisoner* – one of the most challenging and thought-provoking television series of all time – is mainly down to two individuals: Patrick McGoohan who saw the potential and had the drive and ambition to see it through, and Lew Grade, the head of ATV at the time, who gave him the necessary funding. McGoohan convinced Lew Grade to back the new project after deciding he'd had enough of *Danger Man*. During the UK run of *Danger Man*, McGoohan was made a very lucrative offer – the role of James Bond. However, he said no to *Dr. No*, and carried on as John Drake for a while. After six years, McGoohan chose to escape, and failing to get McGoohan to stay on as John Drake, Grade let him pitch his new idea.

McGoohan presented the media mogul with a project outline which included details of the new concept as well as projections and budgets, but Grade brushed it aside and asked him to describe the project in his own words. After McGoohan explained *The Prisoner* with great enthusiasm, Grade struck a deal there and then. 'When you decide to do a production of major significance, it's the quality and the idea of the project that counts. Not "what is it going to cost?" That comes afterwards,' said Grade.

'From the very moment that he said "go" and shook my hand, he never interfered with anything I did and never bothered me. It was marvellous,' recalled McGoohan.

Grade's company ITC had hit on affluent times after achieving great success with series such as *The Saint*, *Gideon's Way* and *Seaway*, so there was money to spare. After agreeing on the extent of the series (McGoohan originally only wanted to do 7 episodes – Grade persuaded him to produce more) *The Prisoner* was eventually made in 1966–67 by McGoohan's own production company, Everyman Films Ltd. Most of the *Danger Man* production team were used for *The Prisoner* and each episode had a budget of around £75,000. McGoohan was reportedly television's highest-paid actor at the time of production. The overall budget is said to have reached a million pounds. This was a much higher figure than the budgets allocated to *The Saint* and other shows of the time, mainly because McGoohan's star status guaranteed high viewing figures, and therefore advertising revenue, whatever project he was involved with. Grade also knew he could rely on McGoohan's international fame to sell the series abroad. In fact, one of the first deals Grade made regarding *The Prisoner* was to pre-sell the series to an American network.

McGoohan must be especially praised for getting *The Prisoner* made. It was one big risk. This was a series which violated all the conventions of television and yet was still expected to appeal to the mass audience who were used to conventional popular entertainment series. In the end, the ratings for *The Prisoner*'s first UK transmission in October 1967 weren't spectacular, but they were certainly more than satisfactory. It was seen as a success and, for a while, it looked like the risk had paid off. However, it would be in the years that followed, after intense analysis of the series, that critics and viewers alike began to take more notice of *The Prisoner*.

CHAPTER TWO
WHERE AM I?

'I wanted to show that one could develop even a very beautiful place without defiling it and, given sufficient care, you could even enhance what was given as a backdrop.'

– Sir Clough Williams-Ellis

'Half of the people who visit Portmeirion for the first time look at it and say "What's it for?" The other half look at it and say "This is stunning!" What the architect who designed it, Clough Williams-Ellis, was trying to do was to show that architecture should be fun. It's a wild fantasy village that conjures up a terrific surreal atmosphere. It's just a joy to be there.'

– David Barrie (Six of One founder)

*T*he *Prisoner* has become synonymous with Portmeirion in North Wales, the real location of the Village, where most of the exterior scenes were filmed. Clough Williams-Ellis's most famous creation, Portmeirion is his own special holiday village built over fifty years on part of his ancestral estate in North Wales. Work began in 1925 and the village was completed in 1973, just in time for Sir Clough's ninetieth birthday. In five decades the site, which he acquired for £5000, had come a long way. Back in 1925, as Sir Clough recalled, Aber Ia – as it was originally called – was 'a neglected wilderness – long abandoned by those romantics who had realized the unique appeal and possibilities of this favoured promontory but who had been carried away by their grandiose landscaping... into sorrowful bankruptcy.'

Patrick McGoohan first came across Portmeirion in 1959 when it was used as a location for the *Danger Man* episode 'View from the Villa'. *The Prisoner*'s script editor, George Markstein, has said the idea to use the place again was triggered by a feature on it in a *The Sunday Times* supplement. After reading the piece, it was decided upon as the location for the Village. Talking about Portmeirion, Markstein describes it as 'a place that was completely and utterly breathtaking... like some Venetian palace, you look another way and it looks like a Bavarian castle. I can see somebody waking up with a bad headache and hangover and standing in Portmeirion and going crazy!'

It wasn't until the final credits of the last ever episode, 'Fall Out', that the filming location of the Village was revealed to viewers: 'In the grounds of Portmeirion, Penrhyndeudraeth, North Wales, by courtesy of Mr Clough Williams-Ellis'. Until then, it was only those who had been there who would have guessed that Number 6's prison had been a small Italianate village in North Wales. However, in hindsight – and after detailed analysis of the episodes – it's clear McGoohan inserted two clues as to the location. In the episode 'Do Not Forsake Me, Oh My Darling', he produces an envelope with the address 'Portmeirion Road' and there's also some Portmeirion Pottery on display at various points in the series (even, in one instance, with the base of one cup showing the company name).

After seeing his creation on the small screen, Sir Clough wrote: 'Patrick McGoohan's ingenious and indeed mysterious television series *The Prisoner*... stands alone for its revealing presentation of the place. When seen in colour at the local cinema, a performance he kindly arranged, Portmeirion itself seemed, to me, at least, to steal the show from its human cast.'

At the first ever Portmeirion *Prisoner* convention in April 1977, many Six of One *Prisoner* appreciation society members were fortunate enough to meet Sir Clough. However, he died a year later, five years after the completion of his stunning village, and content that his dream had been realized. He once described his creation as a 'light opera approach to architecture'.

Forty years ago, travel writer James (later Jan) Morris wrote of Portmeirion:

I can't quite define the effect of Portmeirion; I can only express my own reaction – something between a scoff, a gasp and an ecstasy. The anomalous prodigy is very famous. You can expect to meet almost anyone there, from a retired Prime Minister to a television actor learning his lines. It is hostile only to prigs, bores and despoilers; its eccentricity is all genial; and its charm is partly the sincerity of the lost society with time, money, talent and hospitality to spare. I have a cottage on the hills above, and from my terrace I can just make out the golden ball of Portmeirion on its tower-top, invested by greenery. Sometimes it is the last thing when the sun sets, and as I close my shutters I take it as a reassurance that the philistines haven't won yet, but there is still room in the world for quixotry, and proportion and romance.

Sir Clough Williams-Ellis's ancestral home, Plas Brondanw, five miles from Portmeirion, has now also opened its grounds to the public. However, during the years of building work, Williams-Ellis would spend most of his time at the site of his 'experiment'. He liked to describe his special place as 'a home for fallen buildings'. Since its realization, around a quarter of a million people have visited each season.

Situated on the Lleyn peninsula, near Porthmadog, the site overlooks the Traeth Bay estuary and Cardigan Bay. The village itself is home to nine shops, including the *Prisoner* information centre which is based in Battery Cottage, Number 6's residence in the television series. There is also a

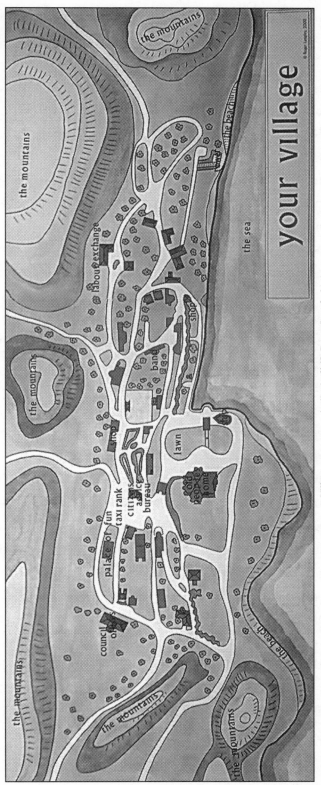

Village map as seen in 'Arrival' (© Roger Langley)

shop selling Portmeirion Pottery seconds. Portmeirion is surrounded by over 70 acres of woodlands known as the 'Gwyllt'. The woods lead down to the beaches of White Sands Bay.

Number 2's headquarters, known as 'The Green Dome' in the series, is the Pantheon, or Dome. The original structure has actually been replaced by a copper dome. The fictional Village hospital is Castell Deudraeth, situated just off the main drive approach to Portmeirion, and the fictional Town Hall is also known as the Town Hall in the non-fictional village.

There were two main shoots in Portmeirion – one in September 1966 and the second in March 1967. Eagle-eyed viewers will notice some slight differences to a couple of Portmeirion's buildings, due to building work. This allows fans to tell whether a scene was filmed in either the March or September shoot. Changes include alterations to the gable above the Ship Shop and a new extension on the same building is also noticeable (in the episodes 'Hammer Into Anvil' and 'Fall Out'). During filming in the Village, the Town Hall was used as the main production office, while all of the equipment was stored in the various cottages. Patrick McGoohan and his family stopped in the very private White Horses cottage. Guest stars were offered Watch House and The Fountain. To save time and money, most actors who played Number 2 never made it up to Portmeirion as it was easier to shoot doubles from the back and dub in dialogue later. Real locals were paid £2 a day for their work as extras and the local Coliseum cinema, in nearby Porthmadog, was even used by production staff to view the day's rushes.

As well as providing the perfect location for *The Prisoner*, Portmeirion has been the setting for various other projects. In 1991, the film *Under Suspicion* starring Liam Neeson was made in the grounds of Portmeirion. *Doctor Who* also used the place as a location for some episodes, as did *Brideshead Revisited* and *The Tripods*. Music videos have also been produced in Portmeirion, most recently 'Allright' by Supergrass. Interestingly, back in the 1960s, the Beatles' manager Brian Epstein would often spend a few weeks in Portmeirion during the summer, usually staying at Gate House. In fact, the main bedroom's wardrobe was built at his request and to his own specification.

Previously, Portmeirion had also been a hiding place for such notable authors as H. G. Wells, George Bernard Shaw, Bertrand Russell and Noel Coward, who wrote his famous comedy *Blithe Spirit* during his stay at The Fountain in the spring of 1941. Coward's companion, Joyce Carey, wrote:

> It was the perfect place... We had a house consisting of two suites one above the other almost on the beach and about fifty yards from the main hotel, and it was there in five days that *Blithe Spirit* was born... The first day to my utter amazement Noel had written at least two thirds of the first act, page after page of neatly typed script, an incredible feat. He said: 'It's always better with me if it pops out like this'.

Portmeirion is obviously an ideal place for fans of *The Prisoner* to meet up with like-minded people. Being together in the very location of their favourite television programme, whether by pure chance or through pre-arranged local group meetings, is a fantastic experience.

After the amount of time he spent trying to escape, it's not surprising Patrick McGoohan hasn't returned to the Village, but that doesn't stop thousands of fans arriving throughout the year to soak up the atmosphere, and it is used for the Six of One annual convention. McGoohan does at least usually send a message either by telephone or fax to organizer Roger Langley, for reading out at the gatherings. Other actors from the series, such as Kenneth Griffith, Alexis Kanner and Mark Eden, have attended the Portmeirion conventions. Most events take place over three days and enable fans, among other things, to play a game of human chess on the same spot where it was played in the episode 'Checkmate' and put questions to the specially invited guests who worked on the series. Many fans arrive dressed as characters from the series. Others prefer to remain individuals.

While Portmeirion often appears as a trademark of the series, in fact the village was only one of several filming locations. Much of the production, including all of the interior scenes, was filmed at the MGM studios in Borehamwood. Sets were constructed for Number 6's cottage, Number 2's chamber and the Control Room, but the best use of the studio lot was for the Western episode 'Living in Harmony', in which an outdoor space became the Western-style town, Harmony.

The opening sequence of the programme uses shots of Abingdon Street underground car park in Westminster and also shots of Number 1 Buckingham Place, Number 6's London home. Footage of Park Lane Garage, Embankment, The Mall, Stag Place and Southampton Row was also used throughout the series. Beachy Head on the Sussex coast was used for both 'Many Happy Returns' and the colourful episode 'The Girl Who Was Death'. For the latter, Southend's Kursaal funfair features heavily; a dress shop in Borehamwood (now a charity shop) is used for scenes with McGoohan and Justine Lord, who played Sonia; and a field in Eltisley, Cambridgeshire, became the cricket ground in the same episode. Finally, the paternoster lift in the GEC building in Borehamwood features in 'Do Not Forsake Me, Oh My Darling'.

Cherish the Past
Adorn the Present
Construct for the Future
– *Sir Clough Williams-Ellis*

CHAPTER THREE
IN PRODUCTION
THE FIRST THIRTEEN

SEPTEMBER 1966 to OCTOBER 1967

*T*he *Prisoner's* success is primarily a matter of style. After finding his perfect location for the Village, McGoohan decided to use some of the best and most experienced television writers and directors. Together with McGoohan's own reputation as an outstanding actor, they helped the programme gather prestige in the pre-production months of early 1966. Other heavyweight actors of the time were also being lined up for parts. *The Prisoner* was already being talked about in the business as it was one of the first television productions to be made in colour on 35mm film.

Writers for the series had to come up with ideas which fitted the standards McGoohan himself had set for the programme. There was to be no romance between McGoohan's character Number 6 and any of the female characters and, as in *Danger Man*, the lead role was to be a serious figure, considerate and a gentleman, despite his incarceration. *The Prisoner* was made in an era when television was seen as a guest in people's homes and this is reflected throughout the seventeen episodes. Number 6 *never* becomes emotionally involved with a woman and always remains a true hero.

All of the seventeen scripts are of an extremely high standard, some written by McGoohan himself, and the rest by other distinguished writers such as Anthony Skene (*Upstairs, Downstairs*), Gerald Kelsey (*The Saint*) and Roger Parkes (*The Onedin Line, Blakes 7*).

Under the pseudonym Paddy Fitz (taken from McGoohan's mother's maiden name, Fitzpatrick), McGoohan wrote the episode 'Free for All', a serious look at the process of democracy. Although made immediately after 'Arrival', it eventually aired as the fourth episode. Next, Anthony Skene wrote the highly surreal 'Dance of the Dead', Gerald Kelsey compared the game of chess with the game of life in his script for 'Checkmate', while Vincent Tilsley delivered, among others, 'The Chimes of Big Ben', a story full of manipulation and mistrust.

David Tomblin took the job of series producer. He was McGoohan's business partner in the Everyman Films venture and had previously worked as an assistant producer on *Danger Man*. He has since gone on to work as second unit director on a number of famous Hollywood films, including most of George Lucas's movies, such as *Raiders of the Lost Ark*. He has also worked on *Return of the Jedi*, *Superman*, Terry Gilliam's *The Adventures of Baron Munchausen* and, more recently, he teamed up with McGoohan again, working as second unit director on Mel Gibson's *Braveheart*.

Directors on the series included Don Chaffey, who directed four episodes including the first two, 'Arrival' and 'The Chimes of Big Ben'. Chaffey had already directed McGoohan in the Walt Disney picture *The Three Lives of Thomasina* (1964) and had also directed some of the *Danger Man* episodes, including 'Colony Three', the episode which many believe inspired *The Prisoner*. Other directors on the series included Pat Jackson and Peter Graham Scott. McGoohan also directed some episodes, as did David Tomblin (see programme credits for full details).

The Prisoner must not, however, be seen solely as McGoohan's own creation. George Markstein, who was script editor, always maintained that the original idea of a spy taken hostage against his will was his own. Markstein co-wrote the first episode, 'Arrival', with the producer, David Tomblin, and remained as the script editor for the first thirteen episodes. He can be seen in a cameo role, sitting behind a desk in the opening sequence of each episode, and makes another brief appearance in the episode 'Many Happy Returns'. It was his job to try to explain to the other writers the essence of the series, while McGoohan worked on some of the more quirky elements of the series. So, in the initial stages, it was McGoohan who began to develop the surreal touches such as Rover, the large white bouncing balloon that acted as the Village guardian.

The original design for Rover was a large motorized device which was produced and taken to Portmeirion for filming. However, because of its loud engine noise and inability to cope with the steps and sand, the crew were forced to use an alternative: the now infamous meteorological balloon.

An Alouette II was chosen as a high-tech looking helicopter belonging to the Village authorities; the Albertus typeface was picked for the credits, while Fenella Fielding was chosen as the cheery voice heard over the Village public address system. She ended up delivering those cosy lines such as 'Good morning. It's another beautiful day.'

Number 6's car was chosen by McGoohan, who had

visited the Lotus factory in 1966. He rejected the Lotus Elan after falling in love with the Lotus 7. The yellow-and-green sports car (KAR 120C) became an integral part of the opening sequence and the series itself.

McGoohan was also responsible for the old-fashioned penny-farthing bicycle, which provided a great contrast to the Village electronic surveillance and other forms of technology. The penny-farthing also became the Village logo used on villagers' lapel badges and on all Village shop merchandise. Therefore, although McGoohan hadn't actually written the script for 'Arrival', as executive producer his influence is easily seen and the surrealism which he inspired is on show from this very first episode.

Grade left McGoohan to get on with it and always admitted he had no idea what the series was about. The deal wasn't signed with contracts but done instead on the strength of a handshake. He gave McGoohan carte blanche. When people at CBS in America first saw the series a few of the network executives telephoned Grade to say that although they loved the series for being different, they didn't understand it. Grade let them visit McGoohan on set. The executives spent two days in Wales but after returning to Grade they told him they were still baffled and demanded to know how on earth he managed to work with McGoohan. Grade replied: 'I never have any problems at all with Patrick McGoohan... I always give in to what he wants!'

By the end of September 1966, the crew were on to their fourth episode, 'Dance of the Dead', in which Number 6 is put on trial for the illegal use of a transistor radio. During a carnival sequence in this strange episode, McGoohan appears in a John Drake-style suit, Number 2, played by Mary Morris, wears a Peter Pan costume, while his observer, Norma West, is dressed like Little Bo Peep. 'I was crazy about him!' recalls West, speaking at a Six of One convention.

> He was the most extremely attractive man. And his unattainability was another thing which was incredibly attractive. You know as soon as you can't have something, you want it. He always had this distance. He'd let you think you were getting to know him, being a friend, and somehow you'd just – not overstep the mark – not go too far – but you'd just do something a little warm or a little brighter than being absolutely cool and he'd snap back immediately. And if you found yourself at a bar ever with him, drinking, and you'd have an ordinary distance then lean forward to say something he'd take a step back and so you'd gradually 'dance' around the bar, moving further and further away!

West also described how Mary Morris (brought in to replace Trevor Howard at the last minute) was as idiosyncratic as McGoohan:

> She was supreme. Superb. I know Trevor Howard was a wonderful, wonderful actor, but I can't help but feel, in this instance, it was very good fortune for 'Dance of the Dead'

that he wasn't available to play it and that Mary played it, because it brought another dimension to it. She was such a powerful, magnetic performer. You wouldn't fail to be completely mesmerized by her, whether you were watching her on the screen or just with her. And a fascinating, eccentric woman. Lovely.

Ian Rakoff, who worked on the script for a later episode called 'Living in Harmony', believes 'Dance of the Dead' is the best *Prisoner* episode by far:

It's taking a piece of trivia and elaborating on it – like buying a bus ticket and making a whole movie out of it. OK, so a guy is caught with an illegal radio but it's not much of a story. But it's well done, it's got such an excellent atmosphere, very English and it really works. From what I can remember it was deemed uncuttable because nobody knew what it was about. John Smith saw it on the shelf, had a go at doing it and made it work.

One of the most complicated episodes to film was 'The Schizoid Man', directed by Pat Jackson in December 1966 and continuing after the Christmas break in January 1967. Terence Feely's script involved Number 6 having to face up to and question himself – literally. His exact double, Number 12, was also played by McGoohan, with stunt double Frank Maher standing in as each character during fight scenes. Maher was required by McGoohan to learn all of the dialogue for both parts, to help with continuity and speed of delivery.

Anton Rodgers, Number 2 in 'The Schizoid Man', recently remarked on the episode's strange plot:

> Terrific. I thought the whole concept was brilliant, not only in terms of the storyline but certainly in the way they filmed it. It was quite unique because there was a gymnasium set, with all of the gymnasium bars around. Of course, in filming, when you do reverse, you have to re-light completely and take all the cameras from that side, turn them round and do it on the other artist. Well, of course, because it was identical all the way round, all you did was change the actor, because the background was all the same. So the lighting was the same, the setting was the same and they saved thousands of pounds by doing that.

Although Rodgers (who also appeared in the *Danger Man* episode 'Yesterday's Enemies') hasn't kept in touch with McGoohan, he's worked with other *Prisoner* actors since and says they all still regard the series as one of the best they've worked on:

> Of all the series that were done then, it was way ahead in my estimation. It asked questions and the scripts were terrific. It was extraordinary. It was one of those things which captured the imagination of the public and they became terribly involved with it and still are to this day.

The only other main thing I remember at the time was that Pat was furious because he was promised distribution in the States and wouldn't accept anything but networking and he had to fight the bosses... but he won! He knew exactly what he wanted. He's a wonderful actor. It's always good working with wonderful actors. If you always had good actors and good directors, we'd all be laughing all the time!

Jane Merrow played the mindreader Alison in 'The Schizoid Man'. Speaking at a *Prisoner* convention in 1994, the actress remarked that her character was different from other roles for women at the time, describing Alison and other female characters in the Village as 'asexual'. 'They were not women, they were just other people there. It was not a man/woman show, so the women were like the men in a way, they were just people.' Merrow also revealed how the actors had to measure up to very high standards: 'We used to get our scripts, probably a week ahead of time, so you had a chance to study the script, learn the lines and come prepared on the first day. And with Pat's shows, you better come prepared, because if you didn't you were in lots of trouble.'

Unlike Anton Rodgers, Merrow *has* kept in contact with McGoohan: 'I met Patrick in '84 when we were both living in Los Angeles. He was a very mellow man then, not the power-house that I remember, which was probably happier for him, but I thought it was rather sad in a way, because he was such a dynamic man.'

At this time during production, in March 1967, the main *Prisoner* theme was recorded by the composer Ron Grainer, the man responsible for the theme tunes for *Doctor Who* and *Maigret*, among others. The session took place at Denham Studios in Middlesex. Music for possible use on the main titles was also composed by Robert Farnon and Wildred Josephs. Farnon's piece, based on the Western *The Big Country*, was rejected outright while Josephs' theme was used as incidental music in 'Arrival'. Grainer also recorded a 'pop' version of his main theme six months later, in September 1967. This jazzed-up piece was released as a single on the RCA Victor label to coincide with the series' initial television screening. Albert Elms composed much of the rest of the incidental music for *The Prisoner* and the rest of the filler music came from the Chappell Music Library, selected by music editor, Eric Mival.

Back on set, as summer approached, trouble was brewing. Differences between script editor (and former journalist) George Markstein and Patrick McGoohan were developing. Markstein always maintained that the Village was based on a real place. He claimed that during the Second World War some government agents who 'knew too much' were sent to an establishment called Inverlair Lodge in a remote part of Scotland for 'a holiday'. Markstein's also suggested that there was to have been a more conventional ending to the series, and that the viewers would have seen a group of villains or 'other side' be revealed as Number 6's captors. McGoohan, however, was focused on the allegorical nature of the series and he was responsible for developing the idea that Number 1 would be Number 6 himself. Nevertheless, Markstein's claim that a real Village did exist has obviously added to the sense of mystery which surrounds the series.

It is clear that McGoohan took Markstein's initial idea and used it to get across his own thoughts and ideas on freedom of the individual and the role of the state in society. It was McGoohan who turned the series into an intelligent allegory as well as a classic television adventure series. Realizing that his reputation was on the line, McGoohan began to take greater control; he put more and more hours in and took over many aspects of production. Behind-the-scenes photographs show that he wasn't timid about operating the camera for many scenes, particularly during the filming of the later episodes.

Writer Vincent Tilsley has told how his original script for 'The Chimes of Big Ben' included a fairly explicit romantic sequence, but was reduced to Number 6 simply stroking Nadia's hair. Similarly, Roger Parkes, who wrote the script for 'A Change of Mind' has told how McGoohan 'desexed' the episode, deleting all references to female character Number 86's crush on Number 6. Not only that, the highly autocratic McGoohan then deleted the director! 'I went down to watch the filming at Elstree,' recalls Parkes.

McGoohan was doing the fight sequences. It was spectacular, they were swinging around. I said 'Where's the director?' and somebody said 'Don't even ask.' McGoohan was doing it. He was pretty high and mighty. I don't recall that he even shook my hand – he may have done, but he certainly didn't consult me. I was told that it was a compliment that he decided to do it. That's what George [Markstein] told me, but it doesn't mean that it's true. It may just have been George being kind. What he said was, 'Don't worry, stop panicking, it's a great thing that he has decided to do it. You're lucky.

Life on set became even more tense when McGoohan sacked another director whose work he wasn't happy with. *Prisoner* cameraman Jack Lowin, who worked on the first thirteen episodes, recalls that staff had a tougher time than on the previous series, *Danger Man*:

It was all getting a bit tense because no episode had been completed and there was considerable pressure from the top, at ITC, to find out what this was going to look like. And so they were putting enormous pressure on Pat, which Pat was resisting, because he was refusing to finish any episode completely. I don't know why; I think he wanted to keep his options open all of the time as to how he was going to do it. He was under pressure and was putting pressure on the crew and people like Dave Tomblin and Bernie Williams because of schedules and they had a problem of scripts arriving and suddenly finding that they needed things – sets, props – that they hadn't got and didn't know anything about until the day before.

In September 1967, just before the first episode 'Arrival' was all set to be transmitted, a press conference was held at MGM studios in Borehamwood to promote the series. McGoohan and other actors from the series, such as Alexis Kanner and Angelo Muscat, were in attendance. McGoohan was dressed in the Kosho outfit and later on changed into his 'Living in Harmony' costume. This was the first time that *The Prisoner* would be seen by anyone other than those involved in the making of the series. It was also the first time that McGoohan would talk about his series. He started as he meant to go on – not revealing much! There were several journalists at the conference who were shown the episodes 'Arrival' and 'The Chimes of Big Ben' as well as *Prisoner* items such as the penny-farthing bicycle and Number 2's globe chair. The original set designs for *The Prisoner* by Jack Shampan were on show as well. These included Shampan's brilliant paintings of the council chambers, the operating room and other sets for the series. After viewing the two *Prisoner* episodes, the journalists understandably wanted to question McGoohan about what they had seen. A question-and-answer session took place but the press had to make do with McGoohan's rather tongue-in-cheek answers. He had the press conference set up so he was actually standing behind prison bars with the journalists standing the other side of them. One dared to criticize *The Prisoner* as having no ongoing story from episode to episode and no real continuity. 'Where's the logic?' the journalist asked McGoohan. 'Let me ask you two questions,' the actor replied. 'You're living in this world? You must answer

"Yes" to that. Do you find it always logical? No? That's your answer to that!' In fact, rather than explaining what *The Prisoner* was all about, the event simply added to the confusion. McGoohan has since continued to put up barriers.

Footage of this press conference may still exist somewhere, as cameras from the television companies covering the event can be seen in stills taken at the time. An 'alternative' version of one episode – 'The Chimes of Big Ben' – has already been found in Toronto by Six of One US co-ordinator Bruce Clark. The discovery was made in the summer of 1986 and shown at a Six of One convention, in Portmeirion, on 30 August 1986. In the alternative 'Chimes', the final credit sequence closes with the world rushing towards the screen and exploding to reveal the word POP. Patrick McGoohan has since condemned the decision to market this as a 'lost' episode. He says it is simply an unedited version. 'There is no lost episode,' he says. But the search is on for any *Prisoner* out-takes. None have ever been discovered.

Already actor, producer, and writer/director on some episodes, by the time his series had been presented to the press, McGoohan had already added the task of overseeing the editing of many episodes to his demanding schedule. Assistant editor Ian Rakoff recalls McGoohan wouldn't usually arrive to view the editors' work until around half past seven in the evening:

He spent more time in the cutting room than most producers or directors would. I thought he was rather magnificent, a thinking, morally aware person and a considerable force. There was just something inside McGoohan that was a lot stronger than most people I've worked with. But it kind of filtered through that he was strung out about everything that was happening on set and that's why I think the situation of John Smith and I just going about our business editing rather appealed to him. He'd quite enjoy turning up with his gins to watch what we were doing.

Rakoff worked mainly on two episodes – 'It's Your Funeral' and 'The General':

I wasn't keen on 'It's Your Funeral' as it was rather run-of-the-mill and had lots of stock footage and library material. 'The General', however, had a very good actor in John Castle, probably one of the best actors in the whole series. What a shame he wasn't used more because he had such an atmosphere of conviction. I don't think any of the other actors, other than McGoohan and Leo McKern, projected that kind of conviction. Although I wasn't enthused by Colin Gordon, the Number 2 in that episode. I found him very lacklustre. In fact I don't know why Leo McKern wasn't used as Number 2 throughout the whole series. It would have been far better to have done that instead of changing the actor each week.

One of the last episodes in the first batch of thirteen to be completed was 'Hammer Into Anvil', which had Patrick

Cargill as the sadistic Number 2 whom Number 6 succeeds in breaking. Cargill spent all of his time in the studio with no location shots at all:

> I do remember it being an enjoyable engagement. As with most film-making, the scenes are often done out of sequence, and it was not very easy to regulate the gradual disintegration of the character. For example, the final scene was filmed first! It was therefore necessary to work backwards, mentally, and sometimes almost sideways before one had the complete mental disintegration of the character in the right order. Not very easy, but very interesting.

It's fair to say that 'Hammer Into Anvil' had more in common with the earlier stories than what was to come. Although the whole series defied convention, episodes such as 'Hammer Into Anvil' were slightly more conventional in plot and narrative than later ones, which became more bizarre as the series progressed. They began to pose *more* questions rather than answer them. This was all down to McGoohan. It is no surprise then that Markstein began to feel left out. After the completion of the thirteenth episode, and as the series was about to be broadcast, Markstein left the series. He was not a happy man, and went on to take every opportunity to make the allegation that it was *he*, and not McGoohan, who created *The Prisoner*. Having written the successful novel *The Cooler*, based on a Kafkaesque concept of people being prisoners of their environment and background, Markstein argues he used the same idea to come up with *The Prisoner*:

> The idea came about at a tea trolley. Patrick McGoohan decided he had got fed up with *Danger Man* and we were all going to be out of a job. So somebody had to come up with an idea to keep the unit together. And what do you do with a secret agent, which is what he was playing in *Danger Man*, whom everybody knew as a secret agent; what kind of part can you find for him that is acceptable to the public and that can make good use of his charisma and so on and so forth? I was very hooked on this Kafkaesque idea of the spy who cannot escape his fate; who cannot resign.

A bitter Markstein also maintained that *The Prisoner* was a direct spin-off from *Danger Man* and that Number 6 was in fact John Drake. He said that everyone was happy for this to be known but McGoohan had changed his stance on the issue because he realized he would have to pay royalties to *Danger Man* creator, Ralph Smart. McGoohan has, of course, claimed otherwise. Whatever Markstein may have believed about the central character, it seems trivial in relation to the allegorical nature of the series imposed by McGoohan. To McGoohan, it didn't matter who Number 6 was. He just happened to look like John Drake. Number 6 was symbolic – of every individual who strives for freedom.

By the end of October 1967, with the completion of the first thirteen episodes, Markstein's departure left McGoohan in total control of the whole production. But inertia was setting in. McGoohan was already the star, producer and co-writer/director. Many of the crew were concerned he was doing too much and, with no script editor, began to wonder how much longer the production could carry on.

CHAPTER FOUR
IN PRODUCTION
THE LAST FOUR

NOVEMBER 1967 to JANUARY 1968

After filming on the first thirteen episodes was completed, it was decided between McGoohan and those at ITC that at least another four would be made – with no script editor. In the event, they were the final four episodes, despite some talk at the time of extending the series to a twenty-six-programme run. In retrospect, it's likely that Lew Grade would have preferred a run of at least twenty-six, possibly thirty – the usual number for a TV series in the 1960s. In fact, McGoohan has always maintained he would only ever have needed seven to do the concept justice. It was only when Grade contacted him, begging for more, that he extended the series. In an interview with Roger Goodman in 1979, McGoohan recalled:

> When I got halfway through filming the seven that I wanted to do, Lew called me, saying he was having difficulty selling it to the network and could I do twenty-six. I said it was impossible and that it wouldn't sustain that amount. So he says, 'Well can you do me *any* more?' I said I'd see what I could do and David Tomblin and I thrashed out another ten stories… most of those were padding anyway.

By the time thirteen had been completed, McGoohan had total control, and this ensured that the final few episodes are probably the most surreal and allegorical of them all. Ironically, it was these last few episodes which would guarantee the whole series cult status in later years, mainly because they are so strange and intriguing that people want to watch them over and over in order to shed new light on what it all means. There aren't many television series of under twenty episodes which are repeated as much as *The Prisoner*.

However, at the time of filming the final episodes, another problem arose when McGoohan committed himself to a new Hollywood film, *Ice Station Zebra*. McGoohan had taken the part for the sake of *The Prisoner*. Saying yes to the role secured financing for four more episodes, but it meant that he had to leave the country to go and co-star with Rock Hudson and Ernest Borgnine in this new blockbuster.

With many of the key *Prisoner* crew gone, McGoohan had to find fresh talent if the series was to continue. Around this time assistant editor Ian Rakoff had been trying his hand at writing, as an experiment, and had told his boss, editor John Smith, that he was keen on coming up with ideas and scripts for possible *Prisoner* episodes. So Rakoff was delighted when Smith said he'd help make it happen: 'John behaved with unusual generosity for the British film industry. He just innocently said to McGoohan that I was a writer and he should read my stuff. I couldn't believe it because I couldn't imagine any other editor going out of his way to do something like that.'

A big fan of Western comic books such as Roy Rogers and Gene Autry, Rakoff came up with a Western which he slotted into the format of the Village:

I remember various people connected with *The Prisoner* said 'You've got people being killed in it, you've got sexual implications! There is no way McGoohan is going to do this.' Although I think Tony Sloman got it right when he assured me McGoohan would love it 'and even if he does-n't, he'll take it, because they haven't got a fresh idea between them'.

On leaving for Hollywood, McGoohan left Rakoff to complete work on the script for his Western and told him he should now report to series producer David Tomblin, a move which frightened the South African-born writer:

McGoohan said that David would look after me and that I'd be in good hands. Of course the only hands David Tomblin thought of were his own and once he'd got this free reign he wanted more of a free reign. He took over and got away with it. And he didn't want me around with McGoohan because I represented probably the very oppo-site of what David Tomblin did while McGoohan was a man on the cusp, caught between different worlds. Tomblin was just so unpleasant and dour that I left.

It soon became clear that McGoohan would have no time to prepare to direct 'Living in Harmony' and that Tomblin had to step in. Not only that, he called in Rakoff and informed him that, as he was now directing, he would also complete the script: 'The final conversation we had about it began with him talking about *my* script, which progressed to *the* script, and by the end of the conversation became *his* script,' recalls Rakoff, who was paid a mere basic screenwriting fee and then left the project. In the end, Tomblin took producer, director and screenwriter credit for 'Living in Harmony' with only a token credit for the original writer: 'From a story by David Tomblin and Ian Rakoff.'

Meanwhile, for the episode 'Do Not Forsake Me, Oh My Darling', the problem of not having McGoohan on set was solved by the ingenious idea of having Number 6's mind being placed into another man's body, that of the Colonel, played by Nigel Stock. Of his role in *The Prisoner* – essentially two parts in one – Stock remarked:

> After the brain-switch, I'm still an Army officer in appearance but mentally the Prisoner. Physically I'm the Colonel; mentally I'm the Prisoner. And as one's mind controls one's actions I am, in fact, portraying Pat McGoohan with all his characteristics. So, I had to think of myself as Pat all the time, behaving in the way he would be doing. Fortunately I've worked with him several times, so I've been able to imitate several of his characteristics, like the way he flicks his fingers and touches his face.

Zena Walker, who played Janet Portland in 'Do Not Forsake Me, Oh My Darling' went down in television history as the first woman to whom a McGoohan character became engaged. But, of course, it was Nigel Stock who was doing the kissing. 'It was something of a disappointment, with all due respects to Nigel,' said Walker. 'I come so near to being the first girl to play really romantic scenes and be embraced by the hard-to-get Patrick McGoohan. On the other hand, it's something of a relief, as I've never met Pat before and I'd probably have been scared stiff. But Nigel and I have had a lot of romantic scenes together in films and television plays.'

While McGoohan was away in the States, Alexis Kanner was also back at Borehamwood, preparing for his role as The Kid in the Western episode, 'Living in Harmony':

David Tomblin and I were preparing the shoot-out sequence, which had me against Patrick, when a telegram arrived. It was from Pat, who said he hoped I was ready because he was taking gun-slinging lessons from Steve McQueen and Sammy Davis Jnr. I think they must've been working on the same lot as Pat. So I was given the Colt Peacemaker to go away and practise with and after a few hours I was getting quicker and quicker. When it came to the day's shoot, everyone on set was having wagers on who would be fastest on the draw – Pat or me! In the end, both guns went off together and nobody could tell who was quicker so we all had to wait for the film to be processed. Finally, the film goes through, twenty-four pictures every second. We counted – Pat took sixteen or seventeen frames, I only took eleven! We all had a laugh about it, including Pat! But everything was such a challenge for him. It's funny really.

Alexis Kanner has also spoken of how all of the *Prisoner* sets at MGM dwarfed Stanley Kubrick's sets for *2001* next door:

As a matter of fact, Pat and I had to share the corridor and we came in one morning and there was a sign saying 'Beware! Dangerous Animal!' I thought it was just another of Pat's jokes because it was put right in front of my door. But it turned out there was a dangerous animal – a leopard – right in the next dressing room!

After directing 'Living in Harmony', Tomblin then directed 'The Girl Who Was Death', a fairytale episode in which a child's storybook comes to life. Justine Lord, who played the title role in this episode, recalls a fairly loose script with a lot of freedom for the actors involved:

David Tomblin seemed to decide things on the day, and I'm sure it evolved between us as we did it – because Patrick didn't join us for a couple of weeks – and what started off as being fairly straightforward evolved, and my costumes and props were almost made up, and the piece developed and built as we went along; in fact, what was originally on paper grew the minute we got on location, and I built on the part as we progressed; and it was shot in sequence. David Tomblin is a marvellous director and a lot of the ideas and development came from him.

Alexis Kanner made another brief appearance (uncredited) in 'The Girl Who Was Death', although he had no lines. He did however have a great time fooling around on the roller-coaster for the amusement park scene, so much so that the cameraman dubbed him a maniac. 'It's amazing what you can do when you're filming that you cannot do when you're a civilian,' explains Kanner. 'I really don't think I could go on one of those rollercoaster rides now! But back then, doing it in front of the whole crew, I was able to stand not only on the seat but up on the bars as well! I wouldn't have been able to do that but obviously the character could do it!'

Kenneth Griffith also appeared in 'The Girl Who Was Death' and played Schnipps, a mad scientist. In the original script Griffith was to have played Hitler, but McGoohan had seen him in a play as Napoleon and decided he should play that part again for this episode of *The Prisoner*. Griffith had already worked with McGoohan on the very last episode of *Danger Man*: 'In my very experienced experience, Patrick McGoohan is one of the most powerful screen personalities I have ever seen,' enthuses the Welsh-born actor.

Anybody can see his power on the screen. Just look at him in the film *Ice Station Zebra* with Rock Hudson. Hudson was a second-rate actor but was a big star. You didn't see Rock Hudson whenever Patrick was on screen! It's impossible to get close to McGoohan because he's such a volatile and private man. I believe he is a devout Roman Catholic and I've often thought Patrick could have been a tremendous Jesuit. He would have been such a force in that order. He is personally detached, so if I praise him I am not pushed by deep affection. I would like to know him better but I haven't seen him for many years.

'The Girl Who Was Death' looked more like an entertaining episode of *Danger Man*, and even the actor Christopher Benjamin appears as Potter again – the same character he'd played in the earlier spy series.

Soon it became clear that Lew Grade was worried that McGoohan and the whole project were going off the rails. The plug was pulled for good and McGoohan had to undertake the enormous task of the final episode, 'Fall Out'. He is said to have still been busy writing this on the weekend before it was filmed. Alexis Kanner was hired again to play Number 48, having already played The Kid in 'Living in Harmony'. This youthful actor brought the energy of the swinging Sixties right into the Village. He'd already starred in the BBC police drama *Softly Softly*, playing the popular character Matt Stone. His first appearance in that show resulted in ratings soaring beyond the twenty-two million mark. But when he left, viewers weren't happy, newspapers fought to bring him back and questions were even raised in Parliament!

Kanner was one of the first to see the script for 'Fall Out':

[Patrick] wrote it on a plane, flying back from Hollywood where he'd just finished *Ice Station Zebra*. But by that point it was like Pat and Dave were making it up as they went along! And to massacre the whole Village and blow the place up in this final script was a serious ending for a pacifist programme. I saw it and said, 'Patrick, we're killing everyone at the end of the show here. Just you and me and Angelo and Leo are going to get out. Isn't this meant to

AMENDMENTS   PAGE 2   " FALL OUT "

INT. DRESSING ROOM. DAY.   11A

EMPTY HANGERS. TAILORS DUMMIES. ONE IS
DRESSED IN P'S ORIGINAL SUIT.

WE HEAR:

                SUPERVISOR'S VOICE
      We thought you would be happier.

CS - P   11B

LOOKING.

INT. DRESSING ROOM. DAY.   11C

TRACKING IN TOWARDS THE SUIT, A HAND REMOVES
IT.

(handwritten annotation)

SUPERVISOR

WE THOUGHT ~~THINK~~ YOU WOULD FEEL HAPPIER AS YOURSELF.

be a series against violence. Isn't it about pacifism and anti-war. We're bumping everybody off!' He laughed and said, 'Yeah, isn't that ironic!' He'd just say, 'Are you ready to start filming, because it's going to be another day of indescribable brutality!'

Kanner's character was very much a youth in rebellion. In order to prepare, he was sent by McGoohan down to Carnaby Street and given a completely free hand to get dressed up. In one scene, the young kid breaks out into a chorus of the Negro spiritual 'Dry Bones', causing chaos in the strange Court of Justice. Kanner recalls how this came about:

Some producer saw 'Living in Harmony', where Patrick and I had the big shoot-out at the end. He came to us and said he had a great idea. It was about The Kid being lost in the jungle. He [the producer] had a script all ready but when he left, Patrick turned to me and said, 'We're not doing that... because that man's hip bone ain't connected to his thigh bone the way yours and mine are.' I asked him what he was talking about and he just turned and said, 'His hip bone is connected to his wallet. Dig? You follow?' and then he grinned and sang 'Dem bones dem bones, dem dry bones' and the next thing I knew it was in the script of 'Fall Out' and I was singing it as an act of rebellion!

Kenneth Griffith, who played the President in 'Fall Out', remembers that McGoohan spent a great deal of time fighting to hold on to his original concept, especially towards the end:

> He was up against the financiers, who would have wanted vulgarity because of worries about their money. People with a lot of money lack perception, except in making money, and lack any sort of creative instinct. All they are interested in is how to make a lousy quick buck. But he's pretty tough and I've heard that in a meeting with Lord Grade [as Lew Grade was now titled], Patrick did end up jumping up and down on a table after a disagreement! In fact, I was complimented by Lord Grade once when he told me I had balls! He said that he'd been looking for a guy with balls ever since Patrick McGoohan left him!

Leo McKern was also back for the conclusion. 'Fall Out' was McKern's third episode. He appeared as Number 2 in all three, one of only two actors asked to return as this character (Colin Gordon being the other). Alexis Kanner recalls that McKern took a lot of persuading to come back after the intense filming and improvization involved in 'Once Upon a Time': 'On his previous episode, Leo was found lying in a foetal position in his dressing room, refusing to carry on. I was the one who had to go and convince him to come back. That's how bad it was.'

This last episode was directed by McGoohan, who made sure that he finished his story off with the great energy and style he had shown throughout *The Prisoner*. He decided to use the thirteenth episode, 'Once Upon a Time', as a penultimate episode, so that 'Fall Out' would become its, and the series', conclusion.

The series ended underground, in a chamber of masked jurors, ready to decide the fate of Number 6. In charge of it all is the President, played by Kenneth Griffith, who says that in the middle of all the chaos, McGoohan asked him to finish writing the President's speech himself. Other than that, Griffith said he was in complete control of everything:

> McGoohan was a tremendous pirate. I remember he would disappear into his room at lunch time – some people say he had to have several stiff drinks just to keep going. But I do recall that when he came back on the set, he was in total command of it all – the concept, the direction and the role he was playing. If you looked at him closely, this tall man was swaying slightly but he never lost a grip on it for a second. In fact, he was pretty terrifying if you got out of line.

During this time, Griffith mentioned to McGoohan that he was obviously tall and handsome and could easily become a big star and make millions: 'But he snapped at me, "No Kenneth! My daughter has a big poster of Steve McQueen in her room. No young woman would stick up a photograph of me!" I think he was wrong but he just rejected the star system. I think he really didn't like being in a business which is so shallow and has such shallow values.'

'Fall Out' was completed two weeks before transmission, in February 1968. Many wonder whether or not there was a real conclusion. The series ends as it began. There is no happy ending and the viewer is left wondering. There are answers to the riddles, but understanding them is another matter! That is a matter for each individual; each will have his or her own interpretation of what McGoohan's final message is.

One of the key moments in the last episode is the death of Rover. Interestingly, the idea for the balloon's demise came about as a result of a thirsty Alexis Kanner's desperate need for a cool drink:

We'd been doing a lot of takes of me running around on the huge 'Fall Out' set and by the end of it I was completely dehydrated and my hands were shaking. One of Pat's stand-ins took me to one side and handed me a cup of tea with five spoons of sugar in it. But it was way too hot so he put a drop of cognac in. I got it to my mouth and found it still too hot. Seeing all of the dry ice and compressed carbon dioxide canisters, I grabbed a cube of dry ice and dropped that in the tea too! As I finally put it to my mouth to gulp it down, the strangest thing appeared on the surface. A bubble appeared from below and grew like something unbelievably evil. Beside it, another and another grew and shrank, until there was a whole mass of them shrinking and dying. It was so horrible I couldn't drink it. I shouted to Patrick who quickly came running over. He then called the prop guy over and told him 'That's it! *That* in close-up is the death of Rover.' Of course, I had to go back to the prop department and spend ages trying to figure out exactly what we'd mixed together. That concoction of tea, milk, five sugars, cognac and dry ice was just sticky enough to do that thing!

Around the time of the filming of these final scenes, there was talk of another series, starring Alexis Kanner and featuring other familiar faces such as the butler, played by Angelo Muscat. In fact, McGoohan wanted the rebellious Kid to continue for another thirty-nine episodes after filming on *The Prisoner* had finished:

He wanted to do a new series – without him but with The Kid, Number 48, as an outlaw and a hunted figure, protected by Angelo, the dwarf. Patrick had a great idea of going to the Tokyo Olympics and wanted to pan along the marathon runners as they entered the stadium and way at the back would be The Kid running along with his top hat and way behind him would be Angelo trying to guard as best he could. It was a charming idea but by the end of filming 'Fall Out' none of us had any real strength to continue.

Interestingly, before he left the series, script editor George Markstein had also talked of his plans for a sequel to *The Prisoner*. His idea was to have Number 6 escape and end up in different parts of the world each week, as in *The Fugitive* and *The Invaders*. Each story would deal with different aspects of personal freedom but at the end of each episode Markstein thought the camera should then pan back to reveal Number 6 had again been watched throughout by Number 2 and his Supervisor back in the Green Dome. This would have been a clever way of extending the series as it would have allowed different location shooting for each episode, while keeping the basic ethos of the series. However, it wasn't to be.

When filming was completed on 'Fall Out', Alexis Kanner received an unexpected gift:

> Pat gave me a photo on the last day of shooting. It was a picture of me holding a bell and he'd written on it, 'Twinkle twinkle little star' which I think was his own unique way of saying thank you and good luck! He also gave me a wonderful picture of the first shot taken by Apollo 7 of the Earth. On it he wrote, 'Till Death Do It Part – Patrick'.

After the screening of the final episode, 'Fall Out', many viewers were angry at the way the series ended. It still wasn't made clear who Number 1 was, although those who looked hard enough found that Number 1 was everyone's own worst enemy: themselves. Who is Number 1? *You* are, Number 6! McGoohan was quoted as saying that 'freedom is a myth'. Number 6 did not escape; he had no freedom. He was a prisoner, as we all are, of our own minds.

The press reviews of the time were mixed. *The Daily Telegraph*'s Peter Knight noted that the series was 'a tense, teasing drama with a difference... certainly no run-of-the-mill pulp thriller, but a stylish, sophisticated, polished production which goes on where *The Avengers* leaves off.' The television critic for the *Daily Mail*, Peter Black, however, criticized the series for the lack of a straightforward narrative. Similarly, the series had critic T. C. Worsley baffled: 'As executive producer, McGoohan bears the whole responsibility and he is such an intelligent fellow that I can only assume that it's I who have missed the point. Perhaps like *The Avengers* it grows on you if you let it.'

Most who watched felt cheated by the highly complex and enigmatic conclusion. This can't have surprised McGoohan, who would have realized that people might not take to the extremely fast editing of the various shots in the last episode. In fact, talking about that final episode, he said, 'I wanted to have controversy, arguments, fights, discussions, people in anger, waving fists in my face.' People were expecting Number 1 to be revealed as some sort of James Bond-type 'baddy'. Others decided that Number 1 was Angelo Muscat's little butler! Such expectations showed the extent to which the television audience had become conditioned to mainstream television shows with predictable endings. *The Prisoner* was radically different. But the audience reaction got out of hand. McGoohan was forced to leave the country after he tired of people accosting him in the streets. He had become a prisoner of his own success.

The television industry has a reputation for being a cruel system which compromises all creativity, but in the 1960s

ITV was prepared to take a chance with *The Prisoner*. Of course, the irony is that nowadays it is likely that the ITV Network Centre, or any other TV network, would run a mile from a script which is as surreal, off the wall and subversive as McGoohan's.

McGoohan and Tomblin's production company, Everyman Films Ltd, failed to produce further shows and filed for bankruptcy in 1974, with debts of around £65,000. In fact, McGoohan had long since left Great Britain, having gone to Switzerland at the end of the 1960s before finally settling in America.

The Prisoner only lasted seventeen episodes, but in that time Patrick McGoohan had managed to get across his ideas about the society in which we live. The themes of the baffling series are still relevant today: the freedom of the individual, the perversion of science and the nature of man.

Intelligent writing, superb acting, innovative ideas, a complex but intriguing plot all combined to create a stunning new look for a TV series... and the novelty still hasn't worn off!

CHAPTER FIVE
EPISODE GUIDE

THE PRISONER – ITC Productions/Everyman Films Ltd

Executive Producer: Patrick McGoohan
Producer: David Tomblin
Script Editor: George Markstein
Production Manager: Bernard Williams
Director of Photography: Brendan J. Stafford
Art Director: Jack Shampan
Theme Music: Ron Grainer
Assistant Directors: Gino Marotta, Ernie Morris
Editors: John S. Smith, Spencer Reeve, Lee Doig,
Geoffrey Foot, Maureen Ackland, Eric Boyd-Perkins
Casting: Rose Tobias Shaw

1. 'Arrival'
2. 'The Chimes of Big Ben'
3. 'A. B. & C.'
4. 'Free For All'
5. 'The Schizoid Man'
6. 'The General'
7. 'Many Happy Returns'
8. 'Dance of the Dead'
9. 'Checkmate'
10. 'Hammer Into Anvil'
11. 'It's Your Funeral'
12. 'A Change of Mind'
13. 'Do Not Forsake Me, Oh My Darling'
14. 'Living in Harmony'
15. 'The Girl Who Was Death'
16. 'Once Upon a Time'
17. 'Fall Out'

1. 'ARRIVAL'

Written by George Markstein and David Tomblin

Directed by Don Chaffey

Number 6 **Patrick McGoohan**

Guest stars:

Virginia Maskell: The Woman

Guy Doleman: Number 2

Paul Eddington: Cobb

George Baker: The new Number 2

With Angelo Muscat, Peter Swanwick, Barbara Yu Ling, Stephanie Randall, Jack Allen, Fabia Drake, Denis Shaw and Oliver MacGreevy.

A Lotus 7 sports car is driven down a deserted runway. A close-up of the determined driver's face shows the viewer the first glimpse of our hero. We will only know him as Number 6. After driving through the streets of central London, he arrives at an underground car park. He walks down a long corridor and bursts into an office. An older man sits at a desk. Number 6 shouts at him and slams down a letter of resignation.

Returning to his London home, Number 6 doesn't realize he has been followed by a sinister-looking undertaker driving a black hearse. As Number 6 packs his suitcase, gas is pumped through the keyhole of the house. He collapses and falls unconscious on his bed.

When he awakes, Number 6 is confused but unaware of his fate. He slowly walks towards his window to open the blinds. The room is an exact replica of his London home, but when he looks up he is stunned by what he sees. The view of the London street has been replaced by the Village.

Number 6 panics. He runs out of his new home to find someone. The place is deserted until he comes across a waitress busy setting tables. She tells him he is in 'The Village'. He wants to make a phone call and so picks up a futuristic phone. An operator asks him for his number. He tells her he doesn't have a number. 'No number, no call', she says and abruptly hangs up. A brightly coloured Mini Moke taxi pulls up but he is told there is only a 'local service'. Number 6 visits the general stores, tries to buy a map, but finds it doesn't extend beyond the Village's boundaries. Back in his new home, he receives a phone call from Number 2 who tells him to come to the Green Dome.

'A lot of people are curious about what lies behind your resignation. You've had a brilliant career. They want to know why you suddenly left.' This dialogue, spoken by the first Number 2, sets the scene for the whole series. *They* want information. If he gives it to them, he will have his freedom. From this point, Number 6 makes a choice not to give in to the Village authorities but to begin a journey to maintain his own identity and individuality. 'I will not make any deals with you. I've resigned. I will not be pushed, filed, stamped, indexed, briefed, debriefed or numbered. My life is my own.'

In this first episode, Number 6 witnesses all the bizarre elements of Village life. He is taken on a helicopter tour by Number 2 who points out that the Village has its own council building, restaurant and graveyard... He sees that the Village is inhabited by nameless, uniformed conformists living a holiday camp lifestyle. He also notices that there is constant surveillance of the Village. This is his prison.

Behind the cheery facade, there is something more sinister. Number 6 witnesses an attack on a man by a huge white bouncing balloon called Rover. Its loud roar causes all Villagers to stop whatever they are doing. The young man who does not stop is suffocated by this menacing Village guardian. Once over, brass band music begins to play again and the Villagers resume their pointless daily lives. Signs urge them to 'Walk on the grass' and others warn them that 'Questions are a burden to others; answers a prison to oneself' or 'A Still Tongue Makes a Happy Life'.

A maid, assigned by Number 2 to extract information from the new prisoner, fails in her task, and it's not long before Number 6 attempts his first escape from the Village. He jumps in one of the taxis and drives down to the beach. He dodges a couple of guardians but is stopped in his path by Rover. He is taken to the Village hospital where he meets up with an old friend by the name of Cobb. They talk about the Village but are separated. Number 6 later overhears a hospital worker saying that Cobb jumped from a window and killed himself.

The following morning Number 6 is discharged from the hospital, now wearing the infamous dark blazer with white piping. He also has a badge on with the number '6' printed on it. In anger, he rips off the badge and tosses it away.

Wanting to know what happened to his friend Cobb, Number 6 goes straight back to the Green Dome, only to find a new Number 2 has taken the place of the first. This new Number 2 reveals very little and only serves to torment Number 6 further by informing him that he is now a number. 'For official purposes, everyone has a number. Yours is number 6.' Number 6 replies, 'I am not a number; I am a person.'

Later, at Cobb's funeral, he meets a woman who tells him that she and Cobb had been planning to escape by using the Village helicopter and a special access device called the 'electropass' which she has found. Number 6 agrees to take Cobb's place in a desperate attempt to escape the Village. With the help of the electropass, he manages to walk past Rover and get into the helicopter. Just as it looks like Number 6 is in command and all set to gain his freedom, the helicopter control lever freezes and steers the craft back towards the Village. Number 6 realizes he has been fooled. The Village authorities are trying to tell him he has no control. But it wasn't the woman who had helped to trick Number 6. It was Cobb who, in the final scenes, is alive and well, back in the Control Room. 'They'll be delighted with you', Number 2 says to Cobb.

Finally, totally defeated, Number 6 walks back into his prison.

In this opening episode, the viewer is introduced to a nightmare. In fact, the situation is so bizarre it could well be Number 6's own dream/nightmare/hallucination. After all, he has just resigned from a very stressful top-secret government position... hasn't he?

'ARRIVAL' Factfile

○ As Number 6, McGoohan gives own date and time of birth on screen: 4:31 a.m., 19 March, 1928.

○ The game of chess is introduced in 'Arrival'. It's significance is highlighted when the ex-admiral tells the woman helping Number 6 to escape: 'We're all pawns.'

○ Originally filmed as '*The* Arrival', an extended 74-minute version of this episode was shot. McGoohan has stated that he never wants the alternative version shown.

○ The first episode was screened on ITV (Midlands and Grampian regions) at 7.30 p.m. on Friday 29 September, 1967.

○ 'Arrival' is the only episode to use the full version of the title sequence and theme music.

○ Number 6's colleague Cobb (Paul Eddington) provides a clue to the initials of the next episode: '<u>C</u>himes <u>o</u>f <u>B</u>ig <u>B</u>en'.

2. 'THE CHIMES OF BIG BEN'

Written by Vincent Tilsley
Directed by Don Chaffey

Number 6 **Patrick McGoohan**

Guest stars
Leo McKern: *Number 2*
Nadia Gray: *Nadia*
Finlay Currie: *The General*
Richard Wattis: *Fotheringay*

With Peter Swanwick, Angelo Muscat, Christopher Benjamin, Kevin Stoney, David Arlen and Hilda Barry.

This second episode begins with an edited down sequence of events taken from 'Arrival' to explain to new viewers how Number 6's situation came about. Indeed, at the start of most episodes we still see Number 6 resign and then awake in the Village. This is followed by an additional dialogue sequence:

Number 6: Where am I?
Number 2:   In the Village.
Number 6: What do you want?
Number 2:   Information.
Number 6: Whose side are you on?

Number 2: That would be telling. We want information.
Information. Information.

Number 6: You won't get it.

Number 2: By hook or by crook we will.

Number 6: Who are you?

Number 2: The new Number 2.

Number 6: Who is Number 1?

Number 2: You are Number 6.

Number 6: I am not a number, I am a free man!

On another beautiful morning in the Village, the announcer's voice is heard over the tannoy system. She encourages Villagers to enter an arts and crafts exhibition. We are then shown the new Number 2, played by Leo McKern, who is determined to find out why Number 6 resigned, but also knows the prisoner is just as determined not to let slip any such information. Watching Number 6 on a surveillance screen in the Green Dome, Number 2 comments, 'He can make even the act of putting on his dressing gown appear as an act of defiance.'

Not surprisingly, Number 6 shows no interest in the arts competition but does play a game of chess with a retired general. Number 2 joins the two men and introduces himself. Later, Number 6 tells the new authority figure he will 'escape and come back and wipe this place off the face of the earth,' which is dismissed as 'paranoid delusions of grandeur'.

Number 6 returns home to meet his new neighbour, Number 8. She tells him her name is Nadia. It is only when he sees her try to escape by swimming out to sea that he begins to trust her. She too is unsuccessful in escaping, stopped by the brute force of Rover. Number 6's feelings for Nadia become clear when he strikes a deal with Number 2. He agrees to enter the art competition and settle into Village life generally if Nadia isn't punished for her escape attempt.

Together, Number 6 and Nadia plan to escape, using the arts competition as a cover. Number 6 builds a boat but tells Number 2 it is a wood carving for entry into the Village competition. Nadia claims to know the location of the Village. She says it is on the Baltic Coast of Lithuania, only thirty miles from the Polish border. Number 6 believes he can use this information to get them both back to Britain.

The two prisoners do manage to escape from the Village. They arrive in Poland, where a fisherman helps to smuggle them over to England and eventually to London. In Number 6's old London office, his erstwhile colleagues greet him, but familiar questioning begins. 'Why did you resign?' they ask. Just as he is about to answer, Number 6 pauses to listen to the chimes of Big Ben. Looking at his watch, which he had set to Polish time, he sees that the chimes match the time on his watch. What about the hour's difference between the two countries? It dawns on Number 6 that he is back in the Village. He realizes, and so now does the television viewer, that it is not going to be that easy. If Number 6 is going to escape, he must do it alone. He must trust no one.

The only consolation is that Number 6 didn't speak. He recognized the Village authorities' plot against him before it was too late. He must now return to his nightmare and keep alive his dream of escape...

Polls in fanzines reveal this to be one of the most popular episodes, possibly due to the appearance of the great actor Leo McKern and his rapport with McGoohan, but it must also be down to the plot. 'The Chimes of Big Ben' combines humour with true dramatic tension. The will he/won't he escape plot explains much of this episode's mass appeal. Later episodes take a much less traditional approach to television plot structure.

'CHIMES OF BIG BEN' Factfile

○ In an alternative version of this episode, at the very end of the final credit sequence, the Earth comes towards the screen with the word 'POP' filling the frame. The alternative version also includes different theme music, composed by Wilfred Josephs.

○ Richard Wattis makes an appearance as one of Number 6's long-standing colleagues. Wattis had previously played McGoohan's boss in the original half-hour episodes of *Danger Man*.

○ Nadia Gray, born of Russian refugees, had just been granted French nationality before appearing in 'Chimes'. For years she'd been a stateless citizen.

3. 'A. B. AND C.'

Written by Anthony Skene
Directed by Pat Jackson

Number 6: **Patrick McGoohan**

Guest stars
Katherine Kath: *Madame Engadine*
Sheila Allen: *Number 14*
Colin Gordon: *Number 2*
Peter Bowles: *A*

With Angelo Muscat, Georgina Cookson, Annette Carrell, Lucille Soong, Bettine Le Beau, Terry Yorke, Peter Brayham and Bill Cummings.

In the Green Dome, we are instantly introduced to a new Number 2. He is jumpy and agitated. We learn of how some Number 2s, notably this one, are more scared of Village authorities and Number 1 than the Villagers themselves. This Number 2 is obviously desperate to break Number 6 because he knows what will happen to him if he doesn't succeed. The viewer is never actually told what happens to unsuccessful Number 2s. It is left to our imagination. However, we do hear Number 2 talk to his superiors over the phone: 'I know sir, yes. I know I'm not indispensable.'

Terrified of failure, Number 2 decides to resort to dream

manipulation. He chooses to use an untested drug, developed by Number 14, which will make it possible to enter into Number 6's dreams and subconscious thoughts. Village technology allows these thoughts to be converted into images on a television screen. Number 2 wastes no time in carrying out the experiment and has Number 14 meet him that night in the laboratory. Meanwhile, Number 6 has already been sent into a deep sleep in preparation for the first attempt. He lies, unconscious, with electrodes and wires stuck to his head. Three separate injections of the drug are possible, says Number 14, but a fourth would be fatal.

Number 2 tells the concerned Number 14 that he thinks Number 6 was going to sell out and that this was the reason for his resignation. He wants to know who he was going to sell to. He thinks it will be one of three people: A, B or C. 'He must meet each one of them. We shall then know what would have happened if we had not got to him first.' Each of the three people will be introduced into Number 6's dreams in the setting of a Paris party, thrown by Madame Engadine.

First a cassette tape marked 'A' is placed into the machine. This character, we are told, used to work with Number 6 before selling out to the other side. Number 2 therefore thinks it is possible that Number 6 talked to him about doing the same. However, the dream actually reveals that Number 6 is hostile towards A, which angers Number 2. His only hope is that B or C may turn out to be more revealing. Number 14 insists that before B is introduced, Number 6 must have twenty-four hours' rest.

During the rest period, Number 6 does notice a red needle mark where he has been drugged and also instantly recognizes Number 14 in the Village. His suspicions are automatically aroused: something is going on and he knows he must now be on the alert. He confronts Number 2 but gains nothing from the encounter. It only serves to add further stress to the life of Number 2 who is finding it hard to cope with Number 6's defiance.

Later, back in the laboratory, Number 6 is once again unconscious. It is time for 'B' to be introduced into his dreams. B turns out to be a woman who is an old friend. This time, much to Number 2's dismay, the drug seems to wear off before anything serious is discussed between the two. Quickly, using the high-tech equipment, Number 14 puts words into B's mouth. 'Why did you resign?' she asks. But this is obviously not in her character and Number 6, even though he is asleep, suspects something. He asks her some very personal questions, such as what is her son called, which she cannot answer. Number 6 promptly leaves the party. Again, twenty-four hours' rest are needed before Number 2 has his last chance with C.

The following morning, Number 6 checks his wrist and discovers the second needle mark. Determined to find out what they are doing to him, he tracks down Number 14 and follows her to the laboratory. After she leaves, Number 6 is left to his own devices. Having seen the files marked 'A', 'B' and 'C', he pieces together the situation. Number 6, determined to outwit them, empties the syringe and fills it with water, realizing that it will be used that night. Sure enough, later they inject him with the now diluted liquid. On the large television screen, Number 6 is back at Madame Engadine's party. To Number 2's surprise, C is revealed to be Madame Engadine herself who wants to introduce Number 6 to her superior. (Of course, it is Number 6 who is now in control, manipulating his own dreams) Number 14 ironically suggests they call this new superior 'D'!

When Number 6 does come face to face with D, he is wearing a mask. Number 6 demands that he take it off. Number 2's excitement turns to despair when the mask is ripped off to reveal... the face of Number 2 himself.

Still influencing his own dream, Number 6 now walks into the laboratory to meet Number 2 and Number 14. He gives an envelope to the Number 2 in his dream. Inside the envelope are travel brochures. 'I wasn't selling out. That wasn't the reason I resigned', says Number 6.

Beaten at his own game, Number 2's experiment has failed. Ominously, his telephone rings.

Although Number 6 has in no way escaped the Village in this episode, he has been victorious in maintaining his dignity and not revealing his secret. Because of this, the viewer feels less uneasy and more hopeful that he might accomplish something even more substantial soon, like gaining his freedom... if such a thing exists.

'A. B. AND C.' Factfile

○ Screenwriter Anthony Skene reused parts of his 'A. B. and C.' script for another TV show – an episode of the BBC series *Counterstrike*.

○ This episode went under two working titles during production: 'Play in Three Acts' and '1, 2 and 3'.

○ Party-goer Georgina Cookson will later appear as a Number 2.

○ Sheila Allen (Number 14) was one of Patrick McGoohan's first leading ladies in *Danger Man*. After *The Prisoner* she spent much of her later career at the Old Vic and in the Royal Shakespeare Company at Stratford-on-Avon.

4. 'FREE FOR ALL'

Written and directed by Paddy Fitz (Patrick McGoohan)

Number 6: **Patrick McGoohan**

Guest stars
Eric Portman: *Number 2*
Rachel Herbert: *Number 58*

With Peter Swanwick, Angelo Muscat, George Benson, Harold Berens, John Cazabon, Dene Cooper, Kenneth Benda, Holly Doone, Peter Brace and Alf Joint.

It's election time in the Village and Number 6 is encouraged to run for the office of Number 2. The current Number 2 says he will help him with his campaign and that, if elected, he will get to meet Number 1. 'You are the sort of candidate we need', Number 6 is told.

Obviously suspicious, Number 6 doesn't accept the offer straight away. But after a while he is caught up in the whole frenzied atmosphere of the election and, thinking he may actually be able to change things, he announces his decision to stand for the position of Number 2.

Immediately, he launches a tirade at the Villagers: 'Unlike me, many of you have accepted the situation of your imprisonment and will die here like rotten cabbages.' Unthinkingly, the Villagers support him, cheering his speech. They even have posters of Number 6's face with 'VOTE FOR No. 6' emblazoned in red. The mindless crowds haven't listened to what he has said but are simply conditioned to love election fever.

Reporters from the *Tally Ho* newspaper take photographs of him and ask questions to which Number 6 replies 'No comment'. Nevertheless, detailed but fabricated answers immediately appear in the next edition of the paper. By this point, Number 6 is becoming increasingly concerned by the attitudes of the voters, who begin to become very attached to him. One in particular is Number 58, specially assigned to Number 6, who follows him wherever he goes. She speaks in a strange foreign accent, which makes it even more difficult for Number 6 to talk to her.

After Number 6 torments a group of councillors with personal questions such as 'Whom do you represent?', 'Who elected you?' and 'Whose side are you on?', Number 2 tells him such intrusion is 'a serious breach of etiquette' and he must now undergo a truth test. This is in fact a session of brainwashing by Village doctors. Number 6 emerges spouting all kinds of political babble, promising, among other things, less work and more play! The faceless Villagers are even more inspired by this rhetoric.

Number 6 wins the election and is pronounced the new Number 2. In his new office in the Green Dome, Number 6 attempts to free his fellow prisoners by shouting over the public address system. 'This is our chance, take it now. I have command. I will immobilize all electronic controls.

Listen to me, you are free to go', he says. He then decides to set himself free. He runs out of the office but is stopped in his tracks by Village guardians who beat him before dragging him back to the Green Dome. The real new Number 2 is waiting there – it is Number 58.

It has all been yet another act. She speaks perfect English. 'Will you never learn?' she asks. She tells him that what he has just had to endure is 'just the beginning' and asks him if he is now ready to speak. There is no reply. Number 6 is taken back to his quarters, having suffered total defeat and humiliation.

All of the optimism of the last episode has been crushed by the events of 'Free For All'. What has been demonstrated is that no one in the Village can ever be certain where power really lies. Real power is hidden.

'FREE FOR ALL' Factfile

- This is the first episode to be written and directed by Patrick McGoohan (under the pseudonym Paddy Fitz, derived from his mother's maiden name, Fitzpatrick).
- Number 6's election poster is a blown-up publicity photo from the *Danger Man* series.
- Although not credited, the Supervisor was played by Peter Swanwick.

5. 'THE SCHIZOID MAN'

Written by Terence Feely
Directed by Pat Jackson

Number 6: **Patrick McGoohan**

Guest stars
Anton Rodgers: *Number 2*
Jane Merrow: *Alison*

With Angelo Muscat, Earl Cameron, Gay Cameron, David Nettheim, Pat Keen, Gerry Crampton and Dinney Powell.

Number 6 is at home, spending an evening with a young girl – although romance is, of course, out of the question. He is helping Alison practise telepathy. Using cards, she is trying to read Number 6's mind. He concentrates on certain shapes on the cards and she tries to guess those shapes, getting them right most of the time. Before the evening is over, Alison accidentally knocks over a bottle which lands on Number 6's hand, bruising one of his fingernails. After taking a few snapshots of Number 6 for a photographic competition and also apologizing for her clumsiness, she leaves.

That night, Number 6 is drugged. Once again, he is to be brainwashed. During the night, he is subjected to electric shock treatment, which forces him to use his left hand rather than his right one.

Number 6 wakes the following morning to find he is in a different apartment. To his amazement, when he looks in the mirror he sees that he now has much darker hair and a moustache. He also discovers that he is left-handed instead of right-handed, and that he likes different foods and cigarettes from before. He takes his jacket from the wardrobe only to find it now has a Village badge with the number 12 on it. He then gets a telephone call from Number 2, who also addresses him as Number 12 and summons him to the Green Dome.

On his way to the Green Dome, other Villagers also address Number 6 as Number 12. Number 2 tells him that it's all part of a conspiracy to break Number 6! The plan is to convince him he is someone else by using an exact double.

Back in his cottage, Number 6 meets the double, and they take part in a variety of tests to prove themselves. But because the real Number 6 has been brainwashed, he cannot perform as he should, so he is not as good a fencer or marksman as he was. Determined to prove himself, Number 6 thinks he can use the mind-reader Alison to demonstrate that he is the true Number 6. However, she ends up being able to read the double's mind better than the mind of Number 6. She also points out that the real Number 6 should have a mole on his wrist. By now, not surprisingly, it is the double who appears to have the mole.

The following morning, Number 6 sees a bruise on his fingernail which is in the centre of the nail. Looking at a photograph of himself taken by Alison, he sees the bruise is at the base of the nail and that the photo was taken on February 10th – the same date his calendar is now reading. The bruise has travelled halfway up his nail overnight! The truth begins to dawn on Number 6. He starts to remember what the Village authorities have put him through.

In an attempt to get back to his original physical state, Number 6 administers more electric shocks on himself, this time to reverse his left-handedness. He then tracks down the impostor. Now in control, Number 6 challenges him and, after getting the better of him in a fight, he manages to get some information out of him. The impostor reveals that his real name is Curtis and that his password is 'Schizoid Man'.

Confronted by Rover, both Curtis and Number 6 give the 'Schizoid Man' password. This confuses Rover and the menacing balloon proceeds to kill Curtis by mistake.

Realizing that he now has the chance to manipulate the situation, Number 6 immediately telephones Number 2. Impersonating Curtis, he says that Rover has killed Number 6. Arrangements are made by Number 2 for him to be helicoptered out of the Village, but Number 6's plan is foiled at the last moment. 'Give my regards to Susan', says Number 2 to Number 6 before his departure. Number 6 agrees to do just that and sets off in the helicopter.

Moments later, he is returned straight back to the Village. Number 2 greets him: 'Susan died a year ago.'

Against all odds, Number 6 has managed to maintain his identity. It took great willpower, but the Village authorities are no closer in finding out why he resigned and must now be wondering what else they can possibly try without really harming him. Their attempts to break his spirit have so far failed. After all the conditioning and brainwashing, Number 6 is still an individual. But for how long? Is it possible to cope much longer? Number 6 knows that if all his resistance is to be worth anything, he must also escape the Village...

'THE SCHIZOID MAN' Factfile

○ This is the only episode in which the menacing white balloon is named as Rover. Number 2 says 'Deactivate Rover' and is later given the news that 'Rover got him'.

○ Curtis's bedtime reading is *The Home–Coming* by Leonard Barnes.

○ Stunt co-ordinator Frank Maher stands in as Number 6's double.

6. 'THE GENERAL'

Written by Joshua Adam (Lewis Greifer)
Directed by Peter Graham Scott

Number 6: **Patrick McGoohan**

Guest Stars
Colin Gordon: Number 2
John Castle: Number 12
Peter Howell: Professor

With Angelo Muscat, Al Mancini, Betty McDowall, Peter Swanwick, Conrad Phillips, Michael Miller, Keith Pyott, Ian Fleming, Norman Mitchell, Peter Bourne, George Leach and Jackie Cooper.

It's another sunny day in the Village and Number 6 is drinking a cup of coffee in the café. A helicopter hovers above the Village but Number 6 seems to be the only one aware of this. Then he notices a young man sitting at another table who is also aware of what is happening. This man is not like the other Villagers but is more alert and less passive. He also looks at Number 6.

A poster shows the face of an intelligent-looking old man with the slogan of 'It can be done. Trust me.' An announcement comes over the public address system. A serious-sounding male voice from the 'General's department' tells all Village students to return to their dwellings immediately because the Professor is about to start his next history lecture.

Number 6 isn't interested and so orders another cup of coffee. A waiter says the café is about to close and advises him that you're never too old to learn. Number 6 starts to talk to the young man, whose badge reveals him to be Number 12. They discuss what appears on another poster which says '100% entry – 100% pass. Speedlearn: A 3-year course in 3 minutes. It can be done!' 'Nothing's impossible in this place', remarks Number 6.

Number 12 suggests that the helicopters overhead are probably after the Professor and leaves Number 6, who decides to take a look for himself. Indeed, there is an orange alert and the Professor is being chased on the beach. Number 6 stumbles across a tape recorder lying in the sand. He presses the play button and hears the voice of the Professor. He hasn't got time to listen to the message so he hides it back in the sand as he is confronted by various Village guardians. He tells them he is just playing truant, but is escorted off the beach and taken back to his cottage.

On entering his home, Number 6 finds that his television set is already switched on. He watches the screen and sees that the Professor is apologizing for being late. He then starts to speak of the wonders of Speedlearn. He says it is 'a marriage of science and mass communication which results in the abolition of tedious and wasteful schooling… a three-year course indelibly impressed on the mind in three minutes.' He also talks of the General, who is behind this educational breakthrough.

After watching the strangely hypnotic lecture for just a few seconds, Number 6 discovers that it is working on him. Later, in a meeting with Number 2, he can give, on command, facts such as the date of the Treaty of Adrianople – September 1829 – and the recognition of Greek independence – 1830. European history hadn't been Number 6's strong point... until now.

Disturbed by what has just happened to him, Number 6 goes back to his cottage and immediately telephones the operator. He asks the same questions which Number 2 had put to him. The operator, gives the same stilted answers, word for word.

Number 6 then decides to go back to the beach to find the tape recorder. When he gets there, he finds that he has been beaten to it because the machine is not where he had placed it and Number 12 is also there. The man hands Number 6 the tape recorder and leaves him to listen to the message. He is not altogether surprised by what the Professor has to say: 'Speedlearn is an abomination. It is slavery. If you wish to be free there is only one way. Destroy the General. Learn this and learn it well. The General must be destroyed.'

The following morning, Villagers are busy testing each other, in preparation for their exams. Meanwhile, Number 6 visits the Professor's wife, who has created various sculptures of people living in the Village, including himself. She isn't very talkative and is frightened of saying the wrong thing. She simply says that she and her husband both came willingly to the Village.

Later that night, Number 12 visits the home of Number 6. They plan to get the Professor's message put out in place of another one of the hypnotic lectures. Number 12 knows where the broadcast studio is and gives Number 6 a special token which will give him access to its control room. It's not long before Number 6 is in position, getting ready to broadcast the Professor's message. However, at the last minute, Number 2, who is watching images from surveillance cameras on the large television viewing screen, notices Number 6. He orders the camera to zoom in to double-check. Security guards are immediately alerted and Number 6 is beaten to the ground and removed from the control room. The official Speedlearn package is broadcast, as the Village authorities had planned it.

Number 2, so proud of what he has achieved, decides to boast a little more and lets Number 6 see the General. The pair arrive, with Number 12, at the Professor's study. At the back of the room are some heavy curtains which draw back automatically to reveal a huge super-computer. Suspicious of Number 12, Number 2 wants to ask the General who it was that helped Number 6 gain access to the control room. He says the computer can answer any question. Seizing this opportunity, Number 6 asks Number 2 if he can feed in a question for the General to answer. Number 6 says the General will not be able to come up with an answer.

Number 2 puts his faith in the Professor's creation and accepts the challenge.

After typing four letters on a piece of paper and feeding it into the General, Number 6 waits with Number 2. The machine begins to hiss and eventually explodes, killing the Professor.

'What was your question?' asks a distraught Number 2. Number 6 replies 'It's insoluble, for man or machine. W.H.Y. Question mark. Why?'

Technological 'miracles' such as computers, which appear to be progressive, are portrayed in this episode as just another form of repression. The kind of soft repression represented by 'Speedlearn' is still all around us and is just as effective as more forceful methods. Children in schools are endlessly taught facts and figures but are they ever taught to look beyond what they have learnt by rote? The Villagers learn through 'Speedlearn', presented through the medium of television. Is McGoohan trying to tell us that television can standardize the way we speak and think?

'THE GENERAL' Factfile

○ Colin Gordon appears for the second time as Number 2.
○ We see the strange underground Village corridors for the first time in this episode.
○ Joshua Adam is the pen-name of Lewis Greifer.

7. 'MANY HAPPY RETURNS'

Written by Anthony Skene
Directed by Joseph Serf (Patrick McGoohan)

Number 6: **Patrick McGoohan**

Guest stars
Donald Sinden: *The Colonel*
Patrick Cargill: *Thorpe*
Georgina Cookson: *Mrs Butterworth*

With Brian Worth, Richard Caldicot, Dennis Chinnery, Joe Laurimore, Nike Arrighi, Grace Arnold, Larry Taylor and George Markstein.

Number 6 wakes up to find that everything has changed. After looking at his watch, he jumps out of bed. He finds that there is no running water and no electricity. Something strange is going on. He goes outside to find a deserted Village. There is silence. He climbs the tower and rings the bell but no one emerges.

Number 6 checks the Green Dome: Number 2's globe chair is empty. Believing there is nothing in the Village to hold him there any more, he plans his escape. He cuts down a few trees and uses the trunks to build a raft. Then he visits the Village general store to obtain food and drink. He even leaves an IOU for ninety-six work units! He also buys a camera so that he can take back some evidence of the Village in the form of pictures. Just before he sets off a loud crash startles Number 6, but luckily it is just a black cat who has knocked over some crockery. In his raft, he slowly sets out to sea.

Using a page from an old edition of the *Tally Ho* newspaper, Number 6, as determined as ever, decides to keep a daily log. However, by 'Day 7', as seen in his logbook, the voyage is beginning to take its toll on Number 6, who is finding it difficult to stay awake. After eighteen days, he finally collapses.

Next, we see two sailors, whose boat has pulled up next to Number 6's raft, busy stealing all of his provisions. When they've got want they wanted, they throw Number 6 into the sea. But without the two men noticing, he uses all of his strength to clamber on to their boat. Inside, he sneaks below deck and, discovering crates of guns, he starts a fire. After a struggle, Number 6 overcomes the two men and ties them up. He then takes control of their boat.

However, it's not long before one of the men struggles free and challenges Number 6 again. Seeing a shoreline in the distance, Number 6 jumps from the boat.

Safely on dry land, Number 6 checks that his roll of camera film is still OK and then looks up at the cliff face he must now climb. Once he is at the top, he meets gypsies who, although rather unfriendly, give him a drink and point him in the right direction.

He finds the nearest road and, to his amazement, peering through some roadside bushes, he sees a good old British bobby! He is back in England. He then jumps on the back of a lorry which takes him to London.

Number 6's first stop is his old London home – 1, Buckingham Place. A maid answers the door but says her mistress is not at home. Suddenly, the familiar sound of Number 6's sports car is heard. It is his Lotus 7, with its familiar registration number – KAR 120C – and it is being driven by a woman. She parks outside the house, gets out and makes her way to the front door. Number 6 tells her that he knows everything about the car she is driving – even the engine number. 'I know every nut and bolt and cog. I built it with my own hands', he says.

She invites him in and introduces herself. She is called Mrs Butterworth and seems very friendly, giving him sandwiches and some cake to eat. Number 6 says his name is Peter Smith. He also tells her that tomorrow, March 19th, is his birthday. She lets him shave and get washed and lends him some of her late husband's clothes. Finally, she even lends him her car and tells him to return soon.

Making his way to his old government office, back in his old car, Number 6 takes a familiar route. It is all eerily familiar. In his office he meets two old colleagues – the Colonel and Thorpe. He shows them his pictures of the Village but they mock his story. After checking the details, however, they say that they are willing to believe him. Based on the information from his daily log, the two men say that the Village is likely to be west of Morocco and south of Portugal and Spain.

The three men organize a search party consisting only of a pilot and Number 6. Together, they fly for a few hours until Number 6 spots the Village. Suddenly, the pilot shouts 'Be Seeing You!' and presses an eject button. Number 6 is parachuted back down to the Village. It is still deserted.

Back in his cottage, after a few seconds, water starts spraying from the shower, a light comes on and the coffee pot starts boiling. The black cat appears in his doorway. Number 6 looks up. It is Mrs Butterworth. This time she is wearing a badge. She is the new Number 2!

'Many happy returns', she says, putting down a birthday cake. Number 6 draws back his curtains. Now the Village is buzzing with many Villagers going about their useless lives to the familiar sound of brass band music.

Number 6's journey in this episode is not just the physical escape from the Village back to his London home. It is also a deeply emotional journey, not only on the part of our hero, but also for us, the viewers. For once, we believe we are getting some kind of perspective as to where his prison has been until all hope is dashed when he arrives back to find escape is not possible. Continuing the allegory, when Number 6 arrives back in London, one of the first images he sees is of bars on the windows of a moving lorry. Surely he now realizes that the whole world really is the Village...

'MANY HAPPY RETURNS' Factfile

○ The standard shot of Number 2 in the opening sequence is omitted to preserve the twist-in-the-tail ending. The opening voice of Number 2 is male, and belongs to actor Robert Rietty, who contributes standard speech throughout the series. Rietty was the voice-over artist famous for his 'This is the voice of the Mysterons' line in *Captain Scarlet*.

○ The birthday cake at the end of the episode has six candles on it.

○ Patrick Cargill, who plays Thorpe in this episode, later appears as Number 2 in 'Hammer Into Anvil'.

○ McGoohan directed the script under the pseudonym Joseph Serf. Many have pointed to the fact that one of the characters in Herman Hesse's great philosophic novel *The Glass Bead Game* goes by the name of Joseph Serf. Hesse's story offered a powerful vision of man's search for personal perfection and social responsibility. Years later, an independent film company considered an adaptation of *The Glass Bead Game* and approached Patrick McGoohan for a role. But the project, also to have starred Terence Stamp and David Bowie, did not get the anticipated funding.

8. 'DANCE OF THE DEAD'

Written by Anthony Skene
Directed by Don Chaffey

Number 6: **Patrick McGoohan**

Guest stars
Mary Morris: *Number 2*
Duncan Macrae: *Doctor*
Norma West: *Little Girl Bo-Peep*

With Angelo Muscat, Aubrey Morris, Bee Duffell, Camilla Hasse, Alan White, Michael Nightingale, Patsy Smart, Denise Buckley, George Merritt, John Frawley, Lucy Griffiths and William Lyon Brown.

Number 6 is in the middle of another tortuous nightmare. A Village doctor is using more shock treatment in the latest attempt to extract the required information from their prisoner. Number 6 has been strapped with all sorts of wires and electrodes by the doctor's assistants who are with him in his bedroom. The doctor is in the Control Room with Dutton, whom he has got to telephone Number 6. Dutton, a former colleague of Number 6, does as he is told.

Number 6 picks up the telephone but refuses to answer any questions. He can take no more of the interrogation and falls back, unconscious. Number 2 walks into the Control

Room, furious that things have gone too far. 'You'll never force it out of this man. He's not like the others', she says.

The following morning, Number 6 wakes to the sound of Village piped music. He seems unaware of what has happened to him during the night. A maid brings him breakfast and a postman delivers an invitation to the Village carnival and dance, to be held the next evening. Later, Number 2 reminds him of the carnival but also asks him to choose from some girls sitting at the café. She says he needs some female company for the evening event. He chooses a nervous-looking young woman who talks to Number 6 but comes across as very shy and eager to get away. Her responses to Number 6 are the usual Village patter: 'Questions are a burden to others; answers a prison for oneself.'

That night, Number 6 is agitated and refuses to sleep. He heads for the beach but is obviously spotted, because Rover is not far behind him. Number 6 is aware of Rover and eventually tires of running. Exhausted, he spends the night on the beach. On waking early the next morning, Number 6 spots a dead man's body lying on the beach. He searches the dead man and finds a wallet containing a photograph and a transistor radio. Number 6 hides the body in a cave and heads for the top of the bell tower to test the radio. It works and picks up various languages. However, he has been watched and Number 2 arrives to confiscate the radio.

As soon as Number 2 is out of the way, Number 6 takes a life-belt from the stone boat down to the dead man in the cave. He writes a note, puts it in the wallet and wraps the whole package in plastic. He attaches the life-belt to the man and pushes him out to sea. His only hope now is that someone will find the body somewhere else and read Number 6's note – a plea for help.

However, turning round, Number 6 is startled to see that a man has been watching him all the time. It is his ex-colleague, Roland Walter Dutton. He explains to Number 6 that he has foolishly told the Village authorities all that he knows and they now see him as 'expendable'. He says that he is now waiting for death.

That evening, Number 6 arrives at the Village carnival and sees that Number 2 is dressed as Peter Pan and the nervous young woman is now Little Bo-Peep. But it's not long before, at a carefully chosen moment, Number 6 decides to leave the carnival. He dons a white coat and starts exploring. Looking like one of the Village doctors, Number 6 is mistakenly given a termination notice, ordering the death of Dutton. After trying unsuccessfully to open several doors, he enters what appears to be a morgue. He sees a body, that of the man who had been dragged into the sea. Suddenly, Number 2 enters and confirms his worst fears. She tells him that they have intercepted the dead body and replaced his note with one of their own – a note which tells of the death of Number 6. His attempt at communication with the outside world has been dashed.

Forced to rejoin the carnival, Number 6 is promptly put on trial. His trial is now the entertainment for the remainder of the night. He is charged with having possession of a radio.

Number 2 will be his defence. Of course, he is found guilty and is sentenced to death.

Number 6 makes his escape but the whole angry mob chase him down the corridors. He finds himself in a room with a teleprinter machine. As it spews paper, Number 6 pulls out its wires. Number 2 enters and tells him that things will remain as they are unless he co-operates. At this point, the teleprinter starts to work again, even though it has just been destroyed by Number 6.

In probably the strangest and most confusing episode of the series, Number 6 is put on trial. But everything is symbolic. The key theme of this episode is death. Although the Village authorities don't want to damage his brain, their aim is to kill his strength. They want his soul. By the end of the episode, things are very bleak for Number 6. Number 2 and her acolytes have certainly weakened his spirit, but is it enough for our hero to give up hope?

'DANCE OF THE DEAD' Factfile

○ Many believe this episode was intended to air as the second in the series. At one point, Number 6 says 'I'm new here' and later, when asked when he was abducted, he replies 'Quite recently.' However, it is likely that many scriptwriters thought or hoped their episode would be second. All had been given the opening script for 'Arrival' and asked to come up with another story. Therefore, it's fair to say 'The Chimes of Big Ben', 'Free for All' and 'Checkmate' could also have been placed second.

○ Denise Buckley played Number 6's personal maid, donning the costume of Marie Antionette for the parade and the Queen Elizabeth I costume for the carnival cabaret. Buckley got the part after mailing 483 pictures of herself to producers and casting directors in the film and television industry. She sent a picture of herself to the studios of The Prisoner, director Don Chaffey saw it and promptly signed her for the role.

○ 'Dance of the Dead' scriptwriter Anthony Skene has admitted being heavily influenced by the surrealism of Jean Cocteau and that the symbolism in his Prisoner episode was therefore 'second-hand'.

9. 'CHECKMATE'

Written by Gerald Kelsey
Directed by Don Chaffey

Number 6: **Patrick McGoohan**

Guest stars
Ronald Radd: *The Rook*
Patricia Jessel: *The Psychiatrist*
Peter Wyngarde: *Number 2*
Rosalie Crutchley: *The Queen*
George Coulouris: *The Man with the Stick*

With Angelo Muscat, Bee Duffell, Basil Dignam, Danvers Walker, Denis Shaw, Victor Platt, Shivaun O'Casey, Geoffrey Reed, Terence Donovan, Joe Dunne and Romo Gorrara.

This episode begins with a sequence of aerial shots of the Village. From the air, the secluded resort looks like paradise, but when the camera zooms in on what we know to be everyday Village life, we are reminded of the nightmare world. Rover, the terrifying guardian, is roaming the Village on another sinister mission.

Despite the rest of the Villagers, who stay very quiet and still, one man is rebelling. A man with a stick continues to walk about, not concerned with Rover's roar. Number 6 sees the man and introduces himself. The two agree to play a game of chess. Everything being possible in the Village, Number 6 soon discovers the game is played with real people, even if most are still the lifeless bunch of Villagers. The game takes place on a giant chessboard on the lawn.

A dark-haired woman greets Number 6 and tells him she will play the Queen, while he will be the Queen's pawn. The man with the stick calls the moves using a megaphone. Suddenly, a man moves to a square without being told to and cries out, 'Check!' These sorts of actions are strictly not allowed and are labelled 'cult of the individual' by the authorities. This man, the Rook, has defied all rules and is promptly escorted to the hospital in a Village ambulance after the game ends.

Later, the old man with the stick talks openly with Number 6. He tells him that the only way to achieve success in the game, and in Village life, is to find out who is on your side and who is not. It is a matter of straightforward human psychology, easily accomplished through simple observation techniques. He is told that Village observers will be uncooperative but Villagers will always unthinkingly follow any orders given to them. By observing people's 'moves' and their general attitudes, one should be able to 'distinguish between the blacks and the whites'. It is only then that any escape plan is worth putting into practice.

Number 6 can see that the Queen is attracted to him and keeps his distance, even when in conversation with the woman. One person Number 6 does try to get to know is the Rook who, after being put through shock treatment and conditioning, is released from hospital. Number 6 and the

Rook become friends and begin to put the psychology plan into practice. However, it is clear that the Rook is still slightly suspicious of Number 6.

They gather a group of residents whom they think they can trust. These include the painter, the chess champion and the shopkeeper, and they will all work together in an escape attempt. The Rook, an electronics expert, puts together a radio signalling device so that they can make contact with ships at sea. The plan is to send out a distress signal in the hope that someone will respond.

Number 2 is involved in another plan to get Number 6 talking. This Number 2 has programmed the Queen to fall in love with him. A reaction transmitter is hidden in a locket and given to the Queen. It is triggered any time that Number 6 tries to escape so that, fearful of losing him, her distress will automatically signal an alarm in the Control Room. However, while engaging in conversation with the besotted Queen, Number 6 notices the locket and asks to look at it. He takes it from her and uses it as part of the escape plan. Taking it from her also means that surveillance of his actions is dramatically reduced. Escape is now possible.

The escape plan is put into action that night and a 'Mayday' distress signal put out. A passing ship, the MS *Polotska*, answers their call. The Rook is instructed to row out to the ship in a raft and Number 6 and his fellow conspirators set off back to the Control Room to immobilize Number 2. They successfully do so. However, the raft has floated back to shore again, unmanned. Number 6 jumps on it and rows out to the boat. Once safely on board, he asks to see the captain. Instead, he is shown a television screen. The face of Number 2 appears. He is no longer tied up. Standing next to Number 2 is the Rook.

'You're one of them', says Number 6 to the Rook. 'I'm not. You are', he replies. Their escape plan has been foiled because of a 'slight misunderstanding'. Because of Number 6's own self-confidence and air of authority, the Rook has decided not to trust him, believing him to be one of the Village authorities.

New methods are shown by the Village authorities in this episode – they simply use Number 6's own authority and self-confidence to defeat him. However, the main theme here is of the game of chess, which is symbolic of life itself. Number 6 is like each and every one of us – a pawn – while the authorities call all of the moves. Until he can find a way out, Number 6, despite all of his protests, is a puppet, along with all of the other Villagers who cheerfully act out the roles that have been assigned to them in the tragic human chess game.

'CHECKMATE' Factfile

- 'Checkmate' was originally made under the working title 'The Queen's Pawn'.
- The shots of the *Polotska* at sea were later used during scenes in 'Many Happy Returns'.
- The human chessboard measured approximately sixty foot square.

EPISODE GUIDE

10. 'HAMMER INTO ANVIL'

Written by Roger Woddis
Directed by Pat Jackson

Number 6: **Patrick McGoohan**

Guest star
Patrick Cargill: *Number 2*

With Victor Maddern, Basil Hoskins, Norman Scace, Derek Aylward, Angelo Muscat, Hilary Dwyer, Arthur Gross, Peter Swanwick, Victor Woolf, Michael Segal, Margo Andrew, Susan Sheers, Jackie Cooper, Fred Haggerty, Eddie Powell and George Leach.

A beautiful young woman, Number 73, is being confronted by the new Number 2. She has obviously just attempted suicide because of the bandages around her wrists. Number 2 wants to know where her husband is, and tries to get her to tell all she knows about his current situation. He even proves to the woman that her husband was cheating on her by seeing another woman.

Number 73 obviously cannot take much more. She screams. Number 6 hears her shrieks from outside and comes running up the stairs and bursts into the room. But he is too late. She has thrown herself from a window, and lies dead. 'You shouldn't have interfered, Number 6. You'll pay

113

for this', warns Number 2. 'No, you will', replies Number 6.

Later on, Number 6 refuses to go and see Number 2, but is dragged to the meeting with his new enemy. As sadistic as ever, Number 2 threatens him with a fencing foil. Then he hits Number 6 hard. They quote Goethe at each other, questioning which of them will be hammer and which will be anvil. Number 2 believes himself to be the hammer. It's up to Number 6 to prove him wrong.

Number 2's red emergency telephone rings, interrupting the pair's dialogue. All we hear is Number 2 nervously explaining himself to his superior. 'Yes, sir... No, sir... Of course, sir,' he says. After Number 6 leaves, Number 2 immediately uses his other telephone, the yellow one, to call the Supervisor: 'Special surveillance on Number 6. Report any unusual activity to me personally', he orders.

Number 6 begins a campaign of planned strange behaviour, aimed specifically at the paranoid Number 2. He goes into the Village record store and listens to the opening chords of six separate copies of Bizet's *L'Arlesienne*; he meticulously makes notes and he also deliberately marks the word 'security' with a question mark on a copy of the Village newspaper the *Tally Ho*. The shopkeeper alerts Number 2 to the peculiar behaviour, and he steps up the surveillance.

Slowly but surely, Number 2 is falling into Number 6's trap. After Number 6 has written two cryptic messages, Number 2 orders an agent to search his home. He finds one of the messages which reads:

TO X.O.4 REF YOUR QUERY VIA BIZET RECORD. NO.
2'S INSTABILITY CONFIRMED. DETAILED REPORT
FOLLOWS. D.6

Number 2 now believes that Number 6 is a plant placed in
the Village to watch over and report on him.

Number 6 continues to inflict this behaviour on Number
2, who is convinced Number 6 will decide his future. It's not
long before Number 2 thinks everyone is part of a mounting
conspiracy against him. Number 6 plants some papers
in the cabin of the stone boat. Desperate to decipher a
message, Number 2 has the blank sheets of paper analysed.
But Number 2 now thinks they are plotting a bid to secure
his downfall. Number 6 also calls the Village psychiatrist
and asks about the 'report' on Number 2. When summoned
to see Number 2 to explain the call, the psychiatrist obviously cannot do so, and is therefore assumed by Number 2
to be a part of the conspiracy. Number 2 even fires one of his
trusted assistants.

Finally, Number 6 sends a cryptic message by homing
pigeon. Number 2 finds it. The message reads: 'VITAL
MESSAGE TOMMOROW. 0600 HOURS BY VISUAL
SIGNAL.' Sure enough, at six o'clock in the morning,
Number 6 walks to the beach and pretends to send a
message in Morse code, using a mirror and the sun.

Number 2 finally turns against his closest servant, the
dwarf butler, who packs his bags and leaves. Now
completely isolated, Number 2 is paid a visit by Number 6

who continues his act, saying that he is a plant and even that Number 2 has sabotaged his investigation. Number 6 says he will not report him – he must report himself. Number 2 picks up the phone: 'I have to report a break-down in control. Number 2 needs to be replaced.' Number 6 leaves, his mission complete.

After Number 6 leaves the distraught Number 2 curled up like a baby in his Globe chair, a huge door closes over the scene. But tellingly, the end sequence still includes prison bars which slam shut on Number 6.

Number 6 has, without a doubt, achieved a lot in this episode. He has completely turned the tables on the Village authority system, going for the all-out persecution of Number 2, who completely loses control. Number 6 finally becomes the Hammer, Number 2 the Anvil. Number 6 has achieved revenge but not escape. He has won his battle with Number 2 – now he must win the battle with Number 1...

'HAMMER INTO ANVIL' Factfile

○ In this episode, Portmeirion's Castle Restaurant provides the exterior for the hospital.

○ Patrick Cargill was an Army officer before he turned to acting. He began his theatrical career as a stage manager and then played minor roles. He also wrote the stage play *Ring for Catty* in which McGoohan starred. Later, Cargill appeared in many films, including the Beatles' *Help!* Cargill also starred in the hit 1968 sitcom *Father, Dear Father*.

○ Director Pat Jackson had previously worked with McGoohan on the *Danger Man* episode 'The Hunting Party'.

○ One of the slogans in the General Stores reads: 'Music makes a quiet mind'.

11. 'IT'S YOUR FUNERAL'

Written by Michael Cramoy
Directed by Robert Asher

Number 6: **Patrick McGoohan**

Guest stars:
Derren Nesbitt: *Number 2*
Martin Miller: *Watchmaker*
Annette André: *Watchmaker's Daughter*
Mark Eden: *Number 100*

With Andre Van Gyseghem, Martin Miller, Wanda Ventham, Angelo Muscat, Mark Burns, Peter Swanwick, Charles Lloyd Pack, Grace Arnold, Arthur White, Michael Bilton and Gerry Crampton.

On another beautiful morning in the Village, Number 6's front door opens automatically. A young blonde woman enters. We see that, as always, the ever-present Village authorities are watching. This time, it is a very good-looking young blond-haired Number 2 and the Supervisor who are surveying the scene on their monitor in the Control Room.

Number 6 is still asleep so the young woman wakes him. He is instantly suspicious of her, as are we the viewers. However, she passes out, but is quickly revived by Number

6 who discovers that she has been drugged. She tells him of an assassination plot and wants his help in preventing it. She also talks of 'jamming' as a way of fighting back. Number 6 refuses to believe the woman's story and she storms out of his room.

We later discover that Number 2 had set up this strange encounter but is disappointed at the outcome. He calls his superiors to assure them that everything will be OK despite a minor delay. It also emerges that Number 2 is trying to dupe Number 6 into unwittingly playing a major role in his plan.

Number 6 visits the Old People's Home and talks to an old man about 'jamming'. The old artist tells him that it is an expression used to describe acts of rebellion and 'plans and developments for all kinds of mischief'. The Village authorities even keep lists of all known jammers, he tells Number 6.

Later, while Number 6 is taking part in a game of Kosho, the strange trampolining game, Number 2's assistant, Number 100, sneaks into the changing room and swaps Number 6's watch with an identical model. Number 6 wins his game of Kosho and goes back to change. He discovers that his watch is not working.

He visits the Village watchmaker's shop to get the watch fixed. While he is there, Number 6 sees an explosive-detonating device on a shelf. He asks the watchmaker about it but the man isn't very forthcoming.

Number 6 learns that the watchmaker is the father of the drugged woman who had woken him earlier that morning.

The woman once again tells Number 6 of the assassination plot and that her father is involved in it. She also says that the victim of the plot will be Number 2. Now convinced that the woman is telling the truth, Number 6 tries to talk her father out of helping with the murder plan, but he will not be persuaded. Number 6 tells him that the Village authorities could take action against all Villagers as punishment, but the watchmaker says that what he is doing is what is needed to 'make them angry enough to fight'.

Number 6 decides to go to the Green Dome to warn Number 2 of the plot, but Number 2 refuses to believe his story. He says that the watchmaker is on the list of 'jammers' and is obviously just trying to be a nuisance. Number 6 leaves the building, not realizing that the whole meeting has been filmed by Number 2.

Later on, Number 6 and the watchmaker's daughter discover that a major Appreciation Day ceremony will soon take place and that the watchmaker has filled a giant seal of approval with explosives. This is to be placed around Number 2's neck during the ceremony.

In a last-ditch attempt to warn Number 2 of the plot, Number 6 goes back to the Green Dome. However, he encounters an old man, the *real* Number 2. This older man recognizes Number 6 and says he knows of the assassination plot. However, he has been warned by the younger Number 2, soon to take over from him after his retirement, that Number 6 would come up with this improbable suggestion. He shows Number 6 some extracts of film which show him warning several Number 2s of the murder plot. The one film of his one visit has obviously been doctored by the younger Number 2 to make Number 6 look like a trouble-maker.

Number 6 protests that the films are fake and finally does convince the retiring Number 2 that there will be an assassination attempt. Number 2 seems resigned to his inevitable fate.

The following day, the ceremony goes ahead and the ritual of the retiring Number 2 handing over the seal of approval to his successor is about to take place in front of the entire Village assembly. The watchmaker is hidden in the bell tower, ready to blow up the retiring Number 2 as soon as the seal is round his neck.

The rebellious Number 6 manages to find the watch-maker just in time and takes the detonating device from him. Number 6 uses the device to turn the tables on the devious young Number 2. After the old Number 2 places the medal over the new Number 2's neck, Number 6 gives the detonating device to the old Number 2, who can now use the helicopter to escape the Village. He won't be stopped because he has the power to detonate the device around the neck of the young Number 2. The escape is successful.

Number 6 has some final words for the terrified young Number 2: 'Came off rather well, I thought. Better than planned. And now you can even look forward to your own retirement and I'm sure they'll arrange something equally suitable for you when the day comes... Be seeing you... won't I?' says Number 6 sarcastically.

Number 6 is once again victorious over the Village authorities in this episode. Not as caught up with escape attempts, at this point in the series he seems to be content with playing the authorities at their own game. However, in scoring another victory, Number 6 is continuously building on his own self-confidence for when his chance of escape comes along...

'IT'S YOUR FUNERAL' Factfile

- This episode was filmed entirely in a studio.
- Derren Nesbitt is the son of the famous British comedian Harry Nesbitt and the nephew of the once-famous Hollywood star, Silvia Sidney.
- Number 100 actor Mark Eden had already worked with Derren Nesbitt and Martin Miller in the *Doctor Who* episode 'Marco Polo'. Eden was later voted 'Britain's Biggest Rat' by the readers of a national tabloid newspaper in the UK. It came after his gripping performance as Alan Bradley in the soap *Coronation Street*. Of his part in *The Prisoner*, Eden has remarked: 'For a villain role opposite Pat McGoohan, it was rather curious to have me wearing a pink jacket!'

12. 'A CHANGE OF MIND'

Written by Roger Parkes

Directed by Joseph Serf (Patrick McGoohan)

Number 6: **Patrick McGoohan**

Guest stars

Angela Browne: *Number 86*

John Sharpe: *Number 2*

With Angelo Muscat, George Pravda, Kathleen Breck, Peter Swanwick, Thomas Heathcote, Bartlett Mullins, Michael Miller, Joseph Cuby, Michael Chow, June Ellis, John Hamblin and Michael Billington

Number 6 is in a tracksuit, busy working out and punching a sandbag in his own improvised outdoor gymnasium in the woods. He doesn't seem to be hurting anyone, just going about his own business. However, two Villagers suddenly appear from behind some bushes and approach him in a somewhat sinister manner. The two men taunt him and pick a fight but eventually lose to the stronger and fitter Number 6. Before they run off they call him anti-social and warn him he will be up before the committee for his actions.

The thugs are right and Number 6 is next seen in the Council Chamber's waiting room. A large poster on one of the walls says 'The Community needs you!' The Council has just finished dealing with Number 93, who is now also in the waiting room ready to hear a verdict on his behaviour. He is told there are signs of disharmony in his behaviour and he must now prove he is once again a suitable member of society. 'Go to the rostrum and confess. We will tell you what to say...' Number 93 then simply proceeds to simply repeat lines fed to him. 'They're right of course. Quite right', he repeats over the loudspeaker so everyone can hear the confession, which includes his admission to being inadequate.

Next it's Number 6's turn to meet the Council. He gets up and enters the Chamber, to be faced with a group of men sitting behind a circular desk. They are obviously not impressed by him but Number 6 just doesn't care what they think. They warn him he is under investigation and that the next meeting will consider his state of health.

After the meeting is adjourned, Number 6 takes a walk through the woods and into the Village. Anyone he tries to greet ignores him. He also reads an article in the *Tally Ho* newspaper with the headline 'Committee Continues Hearings'. Arriving home, Number 6 finds the new Number 2 in his kitchen, eating biscuits. He warns Number 6, 'Failure to co-operate makes one an outcast. Do not defy this committee. If the hearings go against you, I am powerless to help.'

The two men are interrupted by the entrance of a woman whom Number 2 introduces as Number 86. She was once 'disharmonious' but, now reformed, her task is to help

Number 6 begin to join in group activities. However, Number 6 has predictably taken an instant dislike to the woman.

Later, while Number 6 is taking another walk, he comes across a group of Villagers who are talking about 'social conversion'. Number 6 does his best to annoy them, and manages to break up their meeting. They call him a rebel and a reactionary. For continuing this disharmonious behaviour, Number 6 is taken to the Village hospital for examination. While he is there, he witnesses some very distressing aversion therapy. Those who have undergone these experiments appear to have scars on their heads. We learn that these people have been declared 'unmutual' and have undergone 'instant social conversion', an operation he could well soon be subjected to.

Number 6 is indeed declared unmutual, and all the Villagers quickly become hostile and aggressive towards him. Villagers are instructed via the loudspeaker to report any of his antisocial actions. Eventually, Number 6 is totally isolated from all Village life. A large group of Villagers corner him and drag him to the Village hospital.

In the hospital, doctors perform the conversion operation using an ultrasonic beam directed at his frontal lobes. It is explained that the effects of the beam should result in the permanent dislocation of the aggressive frontal lobe of the brain.

Number 6 wakes with a plaster on his forehead. Number 86 prepares a cup of tea for him but Number 6 sees her slip a tablet into his cup. He empties his tea into a flowerpot to avoid being drugged. Number 86 tries the same thing later, but Number 6 foils her again and manages to switch cups. Number 86, now drugged, is hypnotized by Number 6. She reveals that the operation he went through was a fake and the authorities only wanted him to think he had been lobotomized. Still under his spell, she listens as Number 6 begins to feed her instructions. On the fourth chime of the Village bell, she must...

That afternoon, Number 6 approaches Number 2, telling him that he now has peace of mind and is ready to make a public confession from the balcony of the town hall. Of course, Number 2 agrees to this and all of the Villagers congregate in the public square. Number 6 begins his confession but is interrupted. The Village bell begins to chime. On the fourth stroke, Number 86 starts shouting, accusing Number 2 of being unmutual. Number 6 adds to her protests with his own speech: '...you can still salvage your rights as individuals. Your rights to truth and free thought. Reject this false world of Number 2. Reject it. Now!' The Village mob become angry and, turning on Number 2, chase him out of the square.

Despite another victory for Number 6, this episode serves to reinforce just how oppressive the Village authorities can be. Number 6, viewed as a deviant, must be treated and cured according to the powers that be. This episode deals with the idea of removing part of the brain, a frightening treatment in the hands of powerful rulers. We have seen in our own world how Soviet 'dissidents' were defined as mentally ill, confined to institutions and drugged in order to cure their 'sickness'. Indeed the drastic treatments in the world of the Village may have entered our world if one New York psychiatrist had got his way. In 1970, he proposed tests on all six-year-olds to uncover criminal tendencies. The proposals were seriously considered by the American government but never put into practice. This episode shows the Village authorities' great power in destroying individuals, labelling them as sick outcasts. For every Number 6, there are hundreds of thousands of Villagers, mindlessly obeying authority. Who really has the sickness?

'A CHANGE OF MIND' Factfile

○ Angela Brown previously appeared with McGoohan in the *Danger Man* episode 'The Girl in the Pink Pyjamas'.
○ John Sharpe wasn't always an actor – earlier, he'd presented a news programme, *Sharpe at Four*.

13. 'DO NOT FORSAKE ME, OH MY DARLING'

Written by Vincent Tilsley
Directed by Pat Jackson

Number 6: **Patrick McGoohan**

Guest stars
Zena Walker: *Janet*
Clifford Evans: *Number 2*
Nigel Stock: *The Colonel*

With Angelo Muscat, Hugo Schuster, John Wentworth, James Bree, Lloyd Lamble, Patrick Jordan, Lockwood West, Fredric Abbott, Gertan Klauber, Henry Longhurst, Danvers Walker and John Nolan.

The standard opening sequence is absent from the start of this episode. Instead, it begins with a scene which has two Secret Service men in an office. They are examining a set of slides which show various coastal locations – Beachy Head, the White Cliffs of Dover and so on. The men are trying to crack some sort of code which will lead them to Doctor Seltzman, a scientist who has disappeared. 'What's Number 6?' asks one. 'It's Seltzman', replies the other.

The familiar clap of thunder is then heard, followed by the opening credit sequence. However, the music is different

Above: Number 6 in election mode during 'Free For All' (courtesy of Ethel Yeates)

Right: An early scene from 'Arrival' (courtesy of Roger Langley)

Bottom left: Patrick McGoohan in his Elstree office at work on *The Prisoner* (courtesy of Roger Langley)

Bottom right: McGoohan in 'Dance of the Dead' with Rover in the foreground (courtesy of Six of One)

McGoohan reunited with Alexis Kanner in *Kings and Desperate Men*,
where the director's role was reversed, 1983 (courtesy of Alexis Kanner)

McGoohan as Dr Paul Ruth in *Scanners*, 1980 (courtesy of Filmplan)

and the second half of the sequence, the post-credit shots, has been replaced by aerial shots of the Village.

A helicopter flies into the Village. It has brought in the Colonel, who is greeted by Number 2. The Colonel doesn't know it yet but he has been brought in to help with the latest Village plot. In the Green Dome, Number 2 and the Colonel begin to discuss his assignment. It becomes clear that the Village authorities want the Colonel to find Doctor Seltzman, described as 'a great neurologist who became fascinated with the study of thought transfers', a remarkable man who created a technique of mind transplanting, by which the mind of one man can be placed in another man's body.

The Village has managed to steal one of Seltzman's machines. Apparently, they can transplant a mind, but aren't sure if they can safely transfer it back again. The Colonel will try to help the Village authorities find Doctor Seltzman by switching minds with Number 6. This is because Number 6 is known to be the last person to have been in contact with Doctor Seltzman and therefore stands a good chance of locating him again.

Number 6 wakes up in his London home. Things appear to be quite normal, until our hero looks at himself in the mirror. He appears to be a prisoner in a stranger's body. A victim of Village hypnosis, he has no recollection of his time spent in the strange resort. However, some memories begin to filter through.

The doorbell rings. The woman at the door has seen the Lotus 7 parked outside and is desperate to see if her 'darling' is inside. Number 6 instantly recognizes his fiancée, Janet, but of course Janet doesn't recognize him. We learn that the two lovers were engaged to be married before Number 6 was abducted and that he has been gone, at this point, for over a year. We also find out that Number 6 used to work for Janet's father, Sir Charles Portland, one of the men we saw examining the set of slides earlier. He was the man who sent Number 6 on a 'mission' and had refused ever to tell Janet where he was.

Realizing the difficulty of the situation, Number 6 introduces himself as a friend of her fiancé. She leaves, utterly confused. Number 6 smashes his fist into the mirror. He can't bear his new identity.

Number 6 decides that he must see Sir Charles. He storms into the Secret Service offices, demanding to see him. When he does, he tells him of the mind transfer but Sir Charles finds the story difficult to believe. However, he does ensure that one of his men follows Number 6.

Janet's birthday party takes place that evening. Number 6 is there, and convinces her of his true identity after kissing her passionately. He then asks her for a slip of paper he had given her a year ago. It turns out to be a receipt for some photographs he had asked to be developed before his abduction.

Number 6 collects the developed pictures from the camera shop and takes them back to his home. He then uses the photos to crack the code. When put together in their proper order, they show a location: Kandersfeld in Austria. With no time to waste, Number 6 rushes out to his car and drives to Dover. It's not long before he is on the continent, racing through France. Soon, he reaches Kandersfeld. But he has been followed by Sir Charles's men.

Number 6 manages to find Doctor Seltzman, who is now known as Hallen, the local Kandersfeld barber. Seltzman believes Number 6's story and agrees to try and reverse the mind transfer process. However, they are interrupted by one of Sir Charles's men. Ironically, a Village undertaker arrives and gases all three of them!

Number 6 and Doctor Seltzman are taken back to the Village. Seltzman agrees to reverse the transfer process on the condition that he be left alone during the operation. Number 2 agrees, mainly because he knows he has surveillance cameras watching the whole operation anyway.

After intense preparation, we see Number 6, Seltzman and the Colonel all wired up with electrodes connected to each other's heads. Electric sparks crackle and Seltzman collapses. The Colonel gets up, is thanked for his efforts and is then allowed to leave the Village. Seltzman is the next to speak: 'You assured me he was in good health... you must contact Number 1 and tell him I did my duty.' It then becomes clear that the Colonel's mind has been transferred into the dying body of Selzman, while Seltzman's mind is now escaping in the healthy body of the Colonel. Number 6 is now himself again.

Speaking to Number 2, Number 6 has the last word: 'Doctor Seltzman had progressed more than any one of us had anticipated. He can and did change three minds at the same time. He's now free to continue his experiments in peace.'

Following on from earlier episodes, most notably 'The General', this story deals with the theme of the perversion of science. Dr Seltzman is respected for his decision to reject his creation of a devastating invention. He finds he has to come out of retirement to protect people further and is rewarded for his actions. He is the first person we see escape from the Village. Will he be the last?

'DO NOT FORSAKE ME, OH MY DARLING' Factfile

○ Versatile British actor Nigel Stock was perhaps best known for his series *Owen MD* and for his role as Dr Watson in the *Sherlock Holmes* television series.

○ This episode was originally filmed under the working title 'Face Unknown'.

○ With a different pre-credit scene and title sequence for this fourteenth story, many believe this was to have been the first episode in a thirteen-story second series of *The Prisoner*.

○ The letter to Professor Seltzman contains an in-joke – the address contains 'Portmeirion Road' in McGoohan's own handwriting.

○ Part of the set for 'The Girl Who Was Death' is seen in the Kandersfeld set.

○ The GEC's paternoster lift was used as the Headquarters' open elevator.

○ Note the in-joke delivered by café waiter Gertan Klauber: 'Welcome to the Village, Sir.'

14. 'LIVING IN HARMONY'

∗∗

From a story by David Tomblin and Ian L. Rakoff
Written, produced and directed by David Tomblin

Number 6: **Patrick McGoohan**

Guest Stars
Alexis Kanner: *The Kid*
David Bauer: *The Judge*
Valerie French: *Kathy*

With Gordon Tanner, Gordon Sterne, Michael Balfour, Larry Taylor, Monti De Lyle, Douglas Jones, Bill Nick, Les Crawford, Frank Maher, Max Faulkner, Bill Cummings and Eddie Eddon.

In this episode, the standard opening credit sequence is dropped completely. Dressed as a cowboy, Number 6 appears to be free. He is on horseback, sauntering into an old American town.

However, he restates his 'resignation' once more by throwing in his sheriff's badge. He is confronted by a gang of men who beat him up and take him to a town called Harmony. Told by an Indian man not to ask many questions, Number 6 makes his way to the town's saloon. The barmaid, Kathy, offers him a free drink. But the glass is smashed by a bullet fired by an odd-looking young man called The Kid, who now has his gun trained on Number 6. After drinking a second glass given to him by the barman, Number 6 then knocks The Kid out with a single punch.

Next, the elderly Judge, who is obviously running the town, invites Number 6 to his table. The Judge attempts to hire Number 6 for the job as sheriff but is not successful. The townspeople don't understand Number 6's hostility towards Harmony and refuse to help him get out of the place. The Judge decides to lock him up in jail for his own protection.

In jail, Number 6 meets The Kid again. The Kid has now been given the job of guarding Number 6. He also encounters the barmaid Kathy, who is obviously in love with Number 6. Kathy gets The Kid very drunk and gives Number 6 her keys to the jail, thus helping Number 6 to escape. Number 6 gets out of the jail but doesn't get much further. He is captured by the Judge's men and then brought back to the Harmony saloon.

In the saloon, a trial has just begun. But it is not Number 6 who is under the spotlight. It is Kathy who is on trial – for her role in helping him to escape. The court finds her guilty, but the Judge says he will let her go if Number 6 agrees to work for him. To help Kathy, Number 6 puts on the sheriff's badge, although he still refuses to carry a gun – a true moral hero.

The Kid continues to provoke Number 6. He is jealous of Kathy's interest in him, and has already shot one man dead for flirting with her. The people of Harmony don't want The Kid in their town and decide that they want their new sheriff to be armed so he is capable of tackling him effectively.

Number 6 reluctantly agrees to carry a gun. After a fit of jealous rage, The Kid kills Kathy because of her fascination with the new sheriff. Number 6 makes sure he removes his badge, takes his gun and confronts The Kid. In a showdown, he shoots The Kid dead.

Later, the Judge confronts Number 6, who is now back in the saloon with a bottle. Number 6 says he has resigned. He has nothing to lose – Kathy is dead. The Judge says he will kill him first. 'You've got five seconds to make up your mind', he says. The Judge does shoot Number 6 in the back. He falls to the floor and lies dead on the ground.

Number 6 wakes to find himself wearing Village clothes and headphones. There are no real people, just cardboard cut-outs of the characters in Harmony. The piped blazer which has replaced his old cowboy costume confirms that all the events he has witnessed were part of a fantasy sequence, all of which has taken place in his mind. He has not even left the Village. Furious, Number 6 storms into the Green Dome and confronts the Judge, Kathy and The Kid, who are in fact Number 2, Number 22 and Number 8. They all have microphones which they were using to trick Number 6. They've been giving him hallucinatory drugs, in another attempt to make him crack. But Number 2 is very disappointed because the trickery hasn't worked. Nothing seems to have an effect on Number 6.

Number 22 starts crying. She really is in love with Number 6! Suddenly, Number 8 reveals he really is jealous of her interest in him and ends up strangling her to death.

Number 8 then confronts Number 6 again but he is in a complete state of madness by this point, and in a fit of delirium, he kills himself by jumping from the balcony.

Number 6 contemplates all that has just happened. He walks quietly away from the scene.

This episode is yet another shock for the viewer. 'Living in Harmony' is a complete mini-Western film with the only references to the Village near the end. You don't have to be a fan of the genre to recognize the familiar components, such as the saloon room setting and the shootout at the end. McGoohan's use of the Western genre, if only for this one episode, adds to the whole series' mythical status. Film theorists who have analysed the genre argue that Westerns are a myth of contemporary society which also provide a model of social action. By presenting identifiable social types, in a structure of oppositions, viewers can learn how to act by recognizing their own situation in it and observing how it is resolved. Of course, the main oppositions within The Prisoner *are between Freedom and Control, Number 6 and Number 2, Willpower and Force, Escape and Entrapment, Trust and Deception. The Prisoner's model for social action is that to gain the respect of society and your own self-respect, you must be independent, an autonomous and moral individual. The deep social conflicts can only be reconciled through such a model of social action.*

'LIVING IN HARMONY' Factfile

○ The full version of this episode wasn't shown until 1984. Previously, because of censorship problems, drug-related sequences were either deleted or re-edited prior to transmission. Censors weren't happy with the scene showing Johnson's hanging, a fight sequence, and the two scenes where The Kid strangles Kathy. The episode was completely dropped in the first American run of the series.

○ McGoohan's regular stuntman and stand-in Frank Maher was given the part of third gunman in this episode.

○ 'Living in Harmony' has no opening sequence. Against the wishes of McGoohan, British television companies superimposed the words 'The Prisoner' over the first scene.

15. 'THE GIRL WHO WAS DEATH'

Written by Terence Feely

From an idea by David Tomblin

Produced and Directed by David Tomblin

Number 6: **Patrick McGoohan**

Guest stars

Kenneth Griffith: *Schnipps*

Justine Lord: *Sonia*

With Christopher Benjamin, Michael Brennan, Harold Berens, Sheena Marsh, Max Faulkner, John Rees, Joe Gladwin, John Drake, Gaynor Steward, Graham Steward and Stephen Howe.

The usual opening sequence is back but this episode has its own differences. It opens with shots of the pages of a children's storybook being opened. A cricket match is taking place somewhere other than the Village, although the place is also a very typical quaint and bright English village.

On the green, the gentlemen playing don't realize the presence of a beautiful blonde, whom we later discover is called Sonia. After the batsman hits the ball into some bushes, she replaces it with another one. It is a bomb. This ball explodes as soon as the man's bat makes contact with it. It kills the Colonel, Hawke-English.

Number 6, who is dressed in his ordinary clothes, reads about the incident in a newspaper and also finds out from his colleague, Potter, that the Colonel was a Secret Service agent, killed because he was on the trail of a crazy scientist called Doctor Schnipps, who has built a rocket which could destroy London.

Potter's instructions for Number 6 are that he should take over the Colonel's investigation of Schnipps. He accepts the assignment. He must first visit a record shop to receive a special message which he finds recorded on a record disc: 'Find and destroy Professor Schnipps's rocket.'

Back on the cricket pitch, Number 6 is wearing a thick disguise of whiskers and a moustache. Another bomb is put in place, meant for him, but he manages to throw it into the woods before it explodes. It lands where Sonia had previously been hiding. She has left a message for Number 6 to meet her in the local pub.

As he waits for her, Number 6 drinks a glass of beer, only to read a label at the bottom of the glass: 'You have been poisoned.' Quickly, he orders brandy, whisky, vodka, Drambuie, Tia Maria, Cointreau and Grand Marnier, knowing full well the cocktail will make him sick and therefore rid him of the poison. The method works.

Another message leads him to the Turkish baths. After almost suffocating, he then goes on to fight a killer boxer called Karmanski. He is lured to the Tunnel of Love but still fails to find Sonia.

Number 6 then tries to catch up with her by following

her in a sports car. She leads him to a ghost town called Witchwood. Her voice comes over the tannoy system: 'My name is Death,' she says. Number 6 survives the various ordeals Sonia puts him through, including exploding cyanide candles! Finally, Sonia takes the easy option. She hurls grenades at Number 6, shouting, 'Bye bye, lover!'

However, she has not killed Number 6, who makes his way to Schnipps's hideout. We then discover Sonia is Schnipps's daughter. She finds Number 6 and holds him at gunpoint. They reveal that the hideout – the lighthouse they are in – is really a rocket, programmed to take off and destroy London. But Number 6 will be the first to be destroyed as he is sitting in the nose cone!

While Schnipps and Sonia collect their belongings, Number 6 manages to break from his ropes and jumps into a speedboat, leaving the two in the lighthouse. It explodes, killing Schnipps and Sonia.

The action then reverts to the theme of the opening sequence; it is a children's storybook, and we hear Number 6's voice: 'And that is how I saved London from the mad scientist.' In the Green Dome, the new Number 2 (Schnipps) is standing with Sonia. They are outraged their scheme didn't make Number 6 reveal anything. They realize Number 6 will never give anything away, not even to children.

Number 6 tucks the children into bed and turns out the light. Looking at the children, Number 6 says, 'Goodnight children,' and then, looking into the observation cameras,

'...everywhere.' Finally, he places a toy clown in front of the camera.

This is an extremely entertaining episode but rather lightweight compared to the others in the series. Full of action sequences, it is reminiscent of Danger Man, *although it is more of a parody of the spy-adventure genre. Perhaps it is the best example of the type of episode that might have been produced if* The Prisoner *hadn't been cut short after seventeen episodes.*

'THE GIRL WHO WAS DEATH' Factfile

○ This episode was selected for Channel 4's 'Television Heaven' weekend in 1992.

○ The amusement park in 'The Girl Who Was Death' was the Kursaal at Southend, Essex. It no longer exists.

○ The name signs in Witchwood point to more in-jokes – David Dough, Leonard Snuffit and Brendan Bull. Or could that be Tomblin, Harris and Stafford?

○ The *Danger Man* character Potter (from the double 'Koroshi/Shinda Shima' episode) returns in this story, played by the same actor, Christopher Benjamin.

○ The shot used for the 'countdown' sequence was taken from Gerry Anderson's *Thunderbirds* series. It's later used in 'Fall Out'.

○ The Witchwood set can also be seen as the French street in the episode 'A. B. and C'.

16. 'ONCE UPON A TIME'

Written and directed by Patrick McGoohan

Number 6: **Patrick McGoohan**

Guest star
Leo McKern: *Number 2*

With Peter Swanwick, Angelo Muscat and John Cazabon.

The usual full title sequence is used here for the last time. In the Green Dome, Number 2 orders the butler to take away his untouched breakfast tray. Number 6 can be seen on Number 2's monitors pacing up and down in his cottage. 'Relax, why do you care?' says Number 2.

Number 2 picks up the phone and immediately launches into a tirade at the Village authorities. 'I'm not an inmate. You can say what you like. You brought me back here. I told you the last time, you were using the wrong approach. I do it my way or you find somebody else', he says. He then calls Number 6. Our hero still won't co-operate.

After browsing through Number 6's file again, Number 2 makes another phone call, asking for Degree Absolute, a new psychoanalytic test, which lasts for one week only and will thoroughly interrogate Number 6. This will be the last attempt at breaking Number 6 and does seem something of a hasty move. That night, Number 6 is put under electronic hypnosis and Number 2 begins the interrogation process.

Number 2 wakes Number 6 the following morning. 'Want to go walkies?' asks Number 2. He takes Number 6 to the experimentation room. The electronic hypnosis has had serious effects on him. He is now child-like, licking an ice-cream, smiling and reciting the lines of nursery rhymes.

Inside this 'Embryo Room' there is a blackboard, a desk and a rocking horse. But there is still the presence of steel doors which will hold them both in the room for the next week. Number 2 begins to recite passages from William Shakespeare's 'Seven Ages of Man' speech and then writes on the blackboard: 'A – find missing link. When I've found it, refine it, tune it and you will play our game. B – put it together, and if I fail… C – BANG!'

Number 6 is then taken through a series of regression processes – he is the child becoming more mature with each process, while Number 2 is always the authority figure. 'I am your father', says Number 2. They sit at either end of a see-saw, Number 6 reciting 'See Saw Margery Daw'. At every sign of weakness, Number 2 asks why he resigned, but gets nowhere.

The next regression process sees Number 6 as a schoolboy, Number 2 his teacher. Number 6 refuses to conform:

Number 2: Society is the place where people exist together. That is civilization. The lone wolf belongs to the wilderness. You must not grow up to be a lone wolf!

Number 6: No, Sir.
Number 2: You must conform. It is my sworn duty to see
            that you do conform. You will take six... of
            the best.

The Butler has a cane ready but Number 6 protests. He wants twelve of the best!

The exchanges between the two become more and more surreal. In one exchange, Number 6, still refusing to co-operate even when drugged, refuses to say the number six:

Number 2: A, B, C, D, E... Say them.
Number 6: One, two, three four, five.
Number 2: Six.
Number 6: Five.
Number 2: Six.
Number 6: Five.
Number 2: Six.
Number 6: Five.
Number 2: Six.
Number 6: Five.
Number 2: Six.
Number 6: Five.
Number 2: Six.
Number 6: Five.
Number 2: Six of one. Six of one.
Number 6: Five.
Number 2: Six of one. Six of one.

Number 6: Five.

Number 2: Six of one. Six of one.

Number 6: Five.

Number 2: Six of one, half a dozen of the other.

Number 6: Pop goes the weasel.

Number 2: Pop.

Number 6: Pop.

Number 2: Pop.

Number 6: Pop.

Number 2: Pop.

Number 6: Pop.

Number 2: Pop.

Number 6: Pop, pop.

Number 2: Pop.

Number 6: Pop, pop.

Number 2: Pop protect.

Number 6: Protect?

Number 2: Protect pop.

Number 6: Pop.

Number 2: Pop protect.

Number 6: Pop.

Number 2: Protect other people.

Number 6: Protect other pop.

Number 2: Protect other people.

Number 6: Pop.

Number 2: Why?

Number 6: Pop.

Number 2: Why?

Number 6: Why pop?

Number 2: Why?

Number 6: Pop.

Number 2: Why why why?

Number 6: Pop goes the weasel. Half a pound o' tuppenny rice.

Number 2: Why why why why?

Number 6: Half a pound o' treacle. That's the way the money goes.

Number 2: Why why?

Number 6: Pop goes the weasel.

Number 2: Half a pound of pop. Pop.

Number 6: Why?

Number 2: Pop? Pop? Pop? Pop?

Number 6: Pop?

These exchanges wear both men down. Number 6 begins to regain his consciousness and realizes they are stuck in the 'Embryo Room' until one of them breaks. In the final minutes, after a few more exchanges of dialogue, Number 6 manages to lock Number 2 behind the steel bars. The butler now takes his orders from Number 6. The tables are turned and Number 6 interrogates Number 2, effectively swapping roles. Number 6 shouts, 'Die, die, die, die!'

Number 2 collapses. Checking his pulse, Number 6 realizes he is dead. The Supervisor comes in and congratulates Number 6 who, distressed by events, smashes down a glass. The Supervisor leads Number 6 along a corridor and promises to take him to Number 1.

In 'Once Upon a Time' comes the one serious answer Number 6 ever gives to the question 'Why did you resign?' Number 6 answers: 'I resigned for peace of mind.'

This episode is the beginning of the end. It is a tense psychological battle of wills between Number 6 and Number 2. In the end it is about the death of Number 2. Clearly, it is part one of a two-part finale and 'Fall Out' should ideally be watched straight after the viewing of this strong episode. At the end of this episode, Number 6 is beginning to win the battle and is even promised by the Supervisor that he will meet Number 1.

'ONCE UPON A TIME' Factfile

- McGoohan's script for 'Once Upon a Time' closely follows 'The Seven Ages of Man' from William Shakespeare's *As You Like It.*
- The credits list John Maxim as Number 86, although no such character actually appears, as the actor's scenes were cut before transmission.
- In the early scenes, in the discussion of Number 6's childhood experiences, his answers to Number 2 are based on McGoohan's own life experiences.
- This episode was originally filmed under the working title of 'Degree Absolute'.

17. 'FALL OUT'

Written and directed by Patrick McGoohan

Number 6: **Patrick McGoohan**

Guest stars
Leo McKern
Alexis Kanner – *Number 48*
Kenneth Griffith – *The President*

With Angelo Muscat, Peter Swanwick and Michael Miller.

The final glorious episode begins with a montage of sequences from 'Once Upon a Time', making it clear that the two episodes are dependent on each other and should be watched together.

'Fall Out' continues with Number 6 being led down various corridors, including one which is lined with jukeboxes. The Supervisor and the butler lead him through several doors and after walking past a bust of Number 6, the Supervisor says, 'We thought you would be happier as yourself.' The Beatles' 'All You Need Is Love' is playing on one of the jukeboxes. The final door is opened to reveal a court chamber with a masked jury of Defectors, Activists, Pacifists and others.

There is a President who, although dressed as a judge, welcomes Number 6 and begins his speech. He says that

Number 6 has survived the ultimate test and should no longer be referred to as a number of any kind. He should now only be addressed as 'Sir'.

Number 6 is even allowed to sit on a throne to watch the ceremony, the first part of which deals with the resurrection of Number 2. The 'Once Upon a Time' cage in which his body lies emerges and then the President gives the order to 'Resuscitate!' He is laid on an operating table, his face covered with shaving foam and a strange green machine is placed over his head.

The President now discusses three forms of revolt – first, the revolt of youth. Number 48 is brought before the jury, himself charged with revolt. He breaks out into a unique rendition of 'Dry Bones' – 'Collar bone's connected to the neck bone' and so on. He refuses to stop and is found guilty as charged. He is forcibly removed from the room.

Next, brought back to life, Number 2 declares, 'I feel like a new man', and acts accordingly. Now he is friendly, not hostile, towards Number 6 and the butler. Number 2 is found guilty of biting the hand that feeds him. He is therefore the second example of revolt. A complete rebel, he even spits at the mechanical eye of Number 1. Number 2 also exits the chamber.

Finally, there is the revolt of Number 6. But in an impassioned speech, the President applauds Number 6's actions.

He has revolted. Resisted. Fought. Held fast. Maintained. Destroyed resistance. Overcome coercion. The right to be a

Person, Someone or Individual. We applaud his private war and concede that despite materialistic efforts he has survived intact and secure. All that remains is recognition of a man. A man of steel... A man magnificently equipped to lead us, lead us or go.

Number 6 is offered this choice but is also invited to address the assembly. However, when he tries to speak the jury shouts him down. The President thanks him and invites him to meet Number 1.

Number 6 is led through more corridors, going ever deeper underground. On the way, he sees capsules reading 'Orbit 48' and 'Orbit 2', containing Number 48 and Number 2 respectively. After making his way up a spiralling staircase, Number 6 finds himself in a room full of globes. At the back of the room stands a hooded figure. He turns towards Number 6 and hands him a crystal ball. Number 6 drops the ball and rips off the figure's mask. Underneath is the image of Number 6 himself. He chases it out of the room before chaos ensues.

Number 48, the butler and Number 2 help Number 6, confronting and fighting several armed guards. They reach a rocket ship, and press the buttons to launch it. The Villagers are hurriedly evacuated, the rocket is launched and escape now really does look certain.

Next, we see Number 2, Number 48 and Number 6 in the familiar cage, which is mounted on the back of a lorry on the A20. It is being driven by the butler. The three dance to the

'Dry Bones' song. After a while, the lorry stops to let Number 48 get off. Free, he starts hitchhiking down the road. In central London, a policeman pulls the lorry over. Number 2 jumps down and immediately walks over to the Houses of Parliament. Meanwhile, Number 6 and the butler run after a red double-decker bus which takes them to Number 1, Buckingham Place. The door opens automatically…

Number 6 jumps into his Lotus 7. As he drives, the words 'The Prisoner' are seen at the bottom of the screen. Finally, he drives his car down the same runway we see in the opening sequence…

Close your eyes and let the walls of your prison fall away. Walk away from Number 1 and you will be free. But escape is an everyday process. What our hero has taught us is that even though we might think we have freedom, as he appears to have in the end by getting back to his London home, we must constantly question everything around us. But, most importantly, we must never forget to question ourselves.

'FALL OUT' Factfile

- Eight months went by between the filming of 'Once Upon a Time' and 'Fall Out', during which Leo McKern had trimmed his hair and moustache. He also looked a lot slimmer. For continuity, a special resuscitation scene was added to explain Number 2's altered appearance.

- Originally, McGoohan wanted several songs blaring out of the jukebox in a 'wailing cacophony' of sound to include 'Toot Toot Tootsie, Goodbye', 'Hello Dolly', 'Yellow Submarine' and 'Little Boxes'. In the event, only 'All You Need Is Love' was used.

- The Bentley seen overtaking the truck was in fact McGoohan's own car. Meanwhile, KAR 120C in 'Fall Out' wasn't the original Lotus 7 model from 'Arrival', which had been sold to a customer overseas.

- And yet another in-joke... The estate agent's sign in front of Number 6's home read 'Lageu & Son'. John Lageu was the set dresser for this episode.

- In 'Fall Out', viewers finally discover that the location of the Village was 'in the grounds of Portmeirion, Penryhndeudraeth, North Wales, by courtesy of Mr Clough Williams-Ellis'.

- There is no dialogue for the last 15 minutes of this final episode.

- In the final credit sequence, Patrick McGoohan's name is missing. Instead, he is simply billed as 'Prisoner'.

CHAPTER SIX
FREEDOM, THE INDIVIDUAL
AND OTHER THEMES IN *THE PRISONER*

'At this moment individuals are being drained of their personalities and being brainwashed into slaves. The inquisition of the mind by psychiatrists is far worse than the assault on the body of torturers.'

– *Patrick McGoohan, 1968*

Is it possible to be free? Is it really a case of society tolerating the individual or is the individual totally insignificant? In television, the idea of an autonomous individual had never previously been conveyed in such a forceful manner. The questions on individuality that McGoohan presents through *The Prisoner* have precedents in philosophical thought.

In *Mind, Self and Society* (University of Chicago Press, 1934), G. H. Mead argues that our conduct is regulated mostly by the way we take on the attitudes and expectations of others. He regards the structure of society and the individual as inseparable because human beings can only be defined as such within a social context. He stresses that, as individuals in society, we do have room for choice – as to what job we do, which subculture we join and so on.

Peter Berger goes further in *Invitation to Society* (Penguin, 1963), arguing that 'society not only determines what we do but also what we are'. He says that although society is a control system and has the power to exert pressure and coercion on the individual, we don't suffer from this because we actually desire what society expects of us: 'We *want* to obey the rules. We *want* the parts that society has assigned to us.' In other words, we behave in ways that others expect of us, based on previously known identities. For example, if we are known to be funny, we will become wits around people who are expecting that behaviour. Therefore the only choice we have is the choice between certain identities that already exist, those which society has created. Society also creates any knowledge we may have; reality is socially constructed. The structure of our own consciousness is a reflection of the structures of society: 'The walls of our imprisonment were there before we appeared on the scene, but they are ever rebuilt by ourselves. We are betrayed into captivity with our own co-operation.' In Berger's eyes, we are therefore all prisoners who cannot escape from our own personal form of captivity.

McGoohan presents the situation of one individual battling against repressive forces within society. Number 6 is a 'pre-given' subject – independent, rational and autonomous – and it is made clear that he is a hero we should look up to. For the viewers, the image of Number 6 is promoted as desirable and normative. Thus, to be a decent citizen (like the white, middle-class ex-government employee, Number 6) we must be independent, rational and autonomous. Those who lack these qualities, like the Villagers who are weak and passive, are seen as abnormal. However, McGoohan complicates matters. Number 6 *does not* escape. *The Prisoner* isn't therefore just another story which provides us with a simple and unconscious way of defining our role in society. McGoohan doesn't want us to think there is an easy way out. His attacks on the illusion of individual freedom and of the self-sufficient individual can also be discussed in relation to the work of the philosopher Nicholas Rose.

In *Governing the Soul* (Routledge, 1990), Nicholas Rose also rejects the notion that, as individuals, we are capable of thinking for ourselves. He proposes that all we think of as personal, such as our mental states and subjectivities, is actually 'intensively governed'. He claims 'thoughts, feelings and actions may appear as the very fabric and constitution of the intimate self, but they are socially organized and managed in minute particulars'. Rose is convinced that, from the nineteenth century onwards, the measuring and classifying of the human psyche by psychologists and other 'engineers of the human soul' has seriously affected the way we live our lives. He says that psychology emerged as a moral science, constituting what it means to be human and civilized, identifying and administering individuals in relation to a normative image. Therefore, the characteristics that this new language defined as belonging to normal humans – i.e. independence, rationality, self-control and autonomy – have become embedded within social practices such as the school, the family and the hospital which define and regulate us. 'Our thought worlds have been reconstructed, our ways of thinking and talking about personal feelings, our secret hopes have been reshaped. Our very sense of ourselves has been revolutionized. We have become intensely subjective beings.' The logical extension of these ideas is that the criteria provided by the language of psychology, the criteria we use to evaluate ourselves, will also have become embedded in media representations of the normal individual, hence the character of Number 6, which is just one of the many examples of how the media addresses us as subjective individuals. We either identify with the independent (normal) Number 6 or with the highly dependent (abnormal) Villagers or even the parade of evil men and women who take on the job of Number 2.

McGoohan mocks the idea that we can be free individuals throughout. Even the ultimate hero, Number 6, does not manage to escape in the end (even though he might think he has). Though he escapes the Village, he still hasn't escaped from himself. He is always a prisoner of his own mind. However, McGoohan's ideas in *The Prisoner* aren't as bleak as those Rose puts forward. Number 6 does have some victories over the powerful Number 2, even though he may not win the entire battle. As James Donald suggests in *Sentimental Education* (Verso, 1992), there may be some room for individuals to act on the basis that the rules of the game can be changed *while it is being played*, 'however rigged the game may be in favour of some players and against others'. He says that thinking for yourself is not necessarily thinking by yourself. So, if McGoohan was presenting a fictional character and questioning how free he was, was he also, at the same time, questioning the ability of his audience to think for themselves? Is it only now that viewers are beginning to fully understand what *The Prisoner* was all about?

Taking a step out of the confines of the Borehamwood studio lot and Portmeirion, it's worth remembering that Patrick McGoohan was making his series during the summer of love, acid, Carnaby Street fashion and the Beatles. These were changing times and he knew it. McGoohan felt that he should contribute something to this cultural revolution.

'Pat was very concerned that the series would have longevity and he did actually ask whether I felt that the Beatles' numbers would date it or not,' recalls music editor, Eric Mival. 'I said I didn't think they would because even then it was terrific stuff they were turning out and so it seemed as though it would last just as well as the series itself.'

Speaking in a rare interview, on the BBC's World Service in 1996, McGoohan admitted:

> I suppose that the crazy thing that I did fitted into that era to a certain degree and, you know, there were some rather wonderful things happening with the youth and if only the youth had a leader I think that we would have had a great revolution which might have changed the face of the earth for a while, but they didn't have a leader.

However, despite the efforts of the producers and directors, most of the television series made over thirty years ago have not sustained their huge popularity with later generations. But McGoohan succeeded. *The Prisoner* is not just another spy series from the 1960s, but a certified cult classic – a fusion of action adventure, sci-fi, allegory and social satire – with a serious political message that's relevant today. Its popularity is due, in part, to the audience's interest in the fact that society hasn't really changed at all, and that many of the predictions McGoohan set out in *The Prisoner* have been realized.

It was noticeable in the 1960s that society was becoming increasingly grey and controlled. Since then, the Orwellian nightmare of a regulated, highly centralized society has become even more real, and the way we now see *The Prisoner* reflects this paranoia. Perhaps there are parallels with contemporary Britain. In *The Prisoner*, the citizens of the Village were encouraged to vote in an election in which candidates spewed out bland statements and speeches but actually proposed no real policy changes. Number 6 was applauded for running for office on an empty platform. Some people view current British politics in a similar light. And in both the Village and our 'modernized' New Britain, everyone is a prisoner.

As well as being a product of its time, *The Prisoner* was way ahead of its time, looking to the future with a vision not too far removed from the worlds envisaged by Orwell and Huxley. Therefore a strong science fiction element is present throughout the series, expressed through a variety of technologies. The nightmarish Village which holds Number 6 is protected by a menacing guardian – the huge white balloon named Rover, which would suffocate any prisoner who tried to escape. Scientists use hallucinogenic drugs to try to extract the information they are so desperate to obtain. A doctor virtually tortures him in a brutal medical experiment in the enigmatic episode 'Dance of the Dead'. Twenty-four-hour surveillance cameras watch his every move. In this *The Prisoner* was prophetic, as it is not uncommon for all of us today to be watched as we walk through our towns and cities. CCTV will 'Be Seeing You'. In *The Prisoner*, Number 6's life has been recorded and any moment in his history can be viewed on large screens by Number 2 – just as we can now fast-forward, pause or rewind Number 6's life on our own screens with the aid of video. We can watch Number 2 watching Number 6! The first credit card (the Barclaycard) was introduced in 1966, the same year that *The Prisoner* went into production, so McGoohan immediately incorporated it in the series as the Village credit unit. Today, we are all represented by numbers.

The Prisoner tackles other themes which have great relevance today, such as the ideas of ESP, computer technology and the general perversion of science. Episodes such as 'The General' provide a cutting critique of our education system, satirizing the way we all seem to have learned by rote. In this episode, the Professor develops a way of implanting knowledge into the brain in a subliminal fashion called Speedlearn. A university degree in three minutes. As Patrick McGoohan said in a 1985 interview for the Six of One society magazine:

> The right sort of education enables one to think original thoughts. There are people who know something about every subject under the sun. But they are just a reference library. Learning too much stuff, that is closing your mind. You will find all the great inventors – Edison, Bell – I can't think of one who was highly educated. The exploration of their mind wasn't surrounded by too much education. The mind is set free. The innate power of creation was there.

Like Orwell's *Nineteen Eighty-Four* and Huxley's *Brave New World*, *The Prisoner* is an anti-Utopian text. They all present a society in which technology has destroyed human liberty. As in Orwell's totalitarian society, brainwashing is used to control citizens in *The Prisoner*. However, much of McGoohan's series, like Huxley's vision, is taken up with more subtle forms of control and repression. Apart from Number 6 and a few others, the Villagers are sheep-like, conforming to any authority. This seems to have been brought about by a society in which every leisure facility is provided for and which has resulted in the production of a mass of passive, conforming Villagers who lack any real emotion. The Villagers dress in brightly coloured uniforms and their cheerful 'Good Morning' wake-up calls on the public address systems are reminiscent of organized holiday camps in the 1950s. In the Village, every day is a 'beautiful' one. It is a vision of a culture where people have come to love the entertainment and trivia that have destroyed their capacity to think and taken away their freedom. Perhaps this prediction has come true in what we now talk of as the 'Global Village'. Thirty years ago, in 'The Chimes of Big Ben', Number 6 contemplated this terrible possibility. 'The whole earth as the Village?' he asked. 'That is my hope,' replied Number 2.

Indeed, the famous *Prisoner* logo, the symbol of the penny-farthing bicycle, was said by McGoohan to be an ironic symbol of progress. By putting a canopy on the penny-farthing, he's admitted it was an added symbol representing 'security'. In an interview with Roger Goodman, McGoohan stated:

> That's protection. That's safety belts! They're compulsory in some places, you know! The interesting thing is that the people who drive cars most – taxi drivers, truck drivers – don't wear them. I think we should take more risks. How can you get through life without taking risks? Wouldn't life be terribly boring!

In a 1977 TV Ontario interview McGoohan said that the whole series came out of his views on our society's techno-logical advancements: 'I think we're progressing too fast. I think that we should pull back and consolidate the things we've discovered.'

Similarly, in an interview for this book, Kenneth Griffith, who played the President in 'Fall Out', related his views on the Internet to the themes of *The Prisoner*: 'The Internet is death to the human race. I think old Jesus was right... They know not what they do. The generally youthful pursuit of that strange series *The Prisoner* is a very good thing because young people have recognized that *The Prisoner* is a prophecy. Technological "miracles" such as the Internet encourage totalitarianism.' It must be said, however, that many others see the Internet as one of the few tools in our society which allow us freedom of expression, and as having great potential for future 'people power' over the might of corporations.

As we established earlier, *The Prisoner* is allegorical and required a lot more thinking about than most other television series at the time, such as *Man in a Suitcase*, *The Champions* and *The Saint*. However, it seems the majority of the television audience in the late 1960s did not take to this new cultural experience. Perhaps *The Prisoner* is also intentionally allegorical of Patrick McGoohan himself. Number 6 resigns – was McGoohan also 'resigning' from a business which he regarded as shallow and too full of 'show'? Did he realize at the time that, in making such a strange series, he was proving that he himself had individual freedom? *The Prisoner* was not *Danger Man*, it was something radically different. Whatever the intentions, the generally hostile reaction to the final episode, 'Fall Out', led to McGoohan leaving the country. Unlike other 'stars' who have exiled themselves for tax reasons, this was a real and ironic case of the audience actually 'falling out' with the star, and vice versa.

It was only later, when the series was repeated and subsequently released on video, that it attracted a new audience.

CHAPTER SEVEN
THE NEXT GENERATION
KEEPING THE SERIES ALIVE

'Is it any wonder that *The Prisoner* proved a tremendously popular programme? *The Prisoner* can't have become popular because it was obscure and confusing. It must be popular because it cracks the old undemocratic folly of success for the few; because it points the way to comfortable failure for the many.'

– Isaac Asimov (TV Guide, *August 1968*)

To Patrick McGoohan, *The Prisoner* was more than just another job. Having devoted such a big chunk of his life to the project, he was increasingly driven to express his artistic voice in a way no other television project has ever equalled. It's therefore no surprise that during filming he insisted that standards were high. In fact it has been said that McGoohan never allowed the word 'television' to be mentioned on set. This wasn't just another run-of-the-mill ITC/ATV television series and McGoohan didn't want anyone to think along those lines. Quality helped the programme attain credibility and, to this day, there are millions of people around the world who admire *The Prisoner* because of these high standards of craftsmanship. When such standards were coupled with McGoohan's passion and breadth of vision, the result was a series that had the power to captivate the imagination. That is why *The Prisoner* and its imagery have been used on countless occasions in advertising and in media design.

The series has inspired academia as well. In 1978, the Ontario Educational Communications Authority began using *The Prisoner* for study at secondary, college and university levels. The series was presented to students in the way McGoohan intended – as an allegory, symbolic of our own world where the fight for freedom is never-ending.

Students in Ontario weren't the only ones preparing their theses on *The Prisoner*. Arizona State University also had students examine the 'social-psychological concepts' of *The Prisoner* as well as analysing their own identification with the lead character, Number 6.

Another key development in ensuring *The Prisoner* would never fade into obscurity was a phone call to ATV by an interested viewer in 1976. David Barrie, who now lives in Worcestershire, had watched the original screening of *The Prisoner* in 1967 and liked what he saw: 'I was captivated by it. It really struck a chord deep within me. It tore at your heart in some ways. It's radically different. The surrealism, the secret agent in wonderland, the blend of telling an action adventure story on one level and having a deep undercurrent of social comment on a totally different level that if you looked for it, it was there.'

When Barrie saw the repeat screenings on ATV in 1976, all the memories came flooding back:

> It was quite by accident that I stumbled across the late-night repeats on Saturdays. Due to commitments, I always seemed to stumble through the door after the programme had started. It wasn't until the penultimate episode that I caught the announcer, Peter Tomlinson, reading out viewers' comments giving their views on what they thought the series was about. He added that ATV were still trying to contact Patrick McGoohan, unsuccessfully as it transpired.

Hearing these views, Barrie decided he wanted to meet like minds, so that perhaps he could have a conversation with them about *The Prisoner* and find things in common. The local television station was kind enough to put his address out after the last episode, 'Fall Out', and Peter Tomlinson also reminded interested viewers of the address. As Barrie recalls it,

> I nearly fell off my seat. I'd done it! What now? I wondered as I toddled off to bed. I got the answer sooner than I anticipated when, at 2.10 a.m., someone hammered at my door. Somewhat bewildered, I found myself inviting four fine fellows from Sutton Coldfield to come in for coffee. As the kettle was boiling two more enthusiasts arrived from Oxford. Well, here was my half-dozen. How many more? They all departed at dawn, but I was too excited to sleep.

Barrie made sure he was out of the house on Sunday. Sure enough, when he returned, he found several notes stuffed through his letterbox. From Tuesday onwards, bundles of letters started arriving each morning, all asking for further details on *The Prisoner*. Many assumed he had already formed a fan club which was up and running. By the end of the week, Barrie had 400 letters stacked up on his kitchen table. On Monday 16 December 1976, he typed a standard letter which he sent out to everyone. It confidently claimed: 'Not the end – but the beginning.' It also outlined his proposals to launch a *Prisoner* appreciation society but asked everyone to remain patient while he considered the best way to set it up.

Over the next fortnight, Barrie teamed up with two other local fans, Roger Goodman and Judie Adamson, and also attracted the attention of both local and national media. On 23 January 1977 the inaugural meeting of the appreciation society was held, where several interested viewers elected Barrie as Chairman, Judie Adamson as Secretary and Roger Goodman as Treasurer. By this time over 600 letters had poured in over just six weeks and all from one single ITV region. In fact, later on a plug on the Scottish ITV station led to Barrie receiving 1,250 letters in the first mailbag from that region.

At the first meeting, Barrie announced that he wanted the society to help 'expand the audience of *The Prisoner* and to examine the philosophy behind it'. Various issues were debated, including putting pressure on television companies to back a national networked re-screening as well as finding a video company to release the episodes of *The Prisoner*. The idea of local co-ordinators was also raised and a pen-pal system discussed. An annual subscription fee of £1.50 for the year 1977/78 was agreed upon; this was to include four quarterly newsletters and a badge. Names proposed for the appreciation society included: 'Fall Out', 'Rovers', 'Villagers', 'Fellow Prisoners', 'Information Incorporated', 'BCNU', 'The Community', 'Prisoners' Escape Committee', 'Free Man Society', 'Everyman', 'Prisoner's Progress' and 'The Green Dome Society', although, as Roger Goodman pointed out, the latter would have sounded as though the group was dedicated to architectural appreciation. Roger Goodman had come up with the name Six of One, and this was liked by most and later confirmed as the name of the society.

Next, Barrie, Adamson and Goodman wrote to Patrick McGoohan to ask if he'd be the society's Honorary President. Within ten days of mailing him, he'd replied via cablegram and accepted the offer, writing: 'Profoundly grateful to you and the Society for your interest and understanding. Am honoured to accept Honorary Presidency. Blessings to you all. Half a dozen of the other. Be Seeing You.'

In the following few weeks, a deal was reached with ITC, who were glad a society was being set up because for years viewers' correspondence regarding *The Prisoner* had always been forwarded from television companies to ITC, the original producers. Queries had ranged from viewers wanting Patrick McGoohan's address to requests for a Number 6 badge, and one lady even wrote in to ask for the knitting pattern for the cardigan worn by the villain in the episode 'Hammer Into Anvil'!

After getting ITC on board, Barrie then successfully liased with the people at Portmeirion and organized the first Six of One convention, which was held on the weekend of 17 April 1977, with a further one a year later, the weekend of 28 April 1978. Unfortunately, both Judie Adamson and the creator of the Village, Sir Clough Williams-Ellis, had died just two weeks earlier.

For a long time, the society was run from the homes of Barrie, Goodman and Adamson in Cheltenham. In a short space of time, Goodman and Adamson had risen to the surface as the people with the time, ability and acumen to run the service. These talented individuals organized files and databases and looked after the administration side of the appreciation society, including the organization of the design, production and distribution of the first mailings and newsletters. Around this time, the society's membership total stood at 2,000, following several regional ITV screenings. With improved finances, the society was able to organise more events and release various merchandise items to members.

'Virtually everybody we got in touch with – Patrick, Kenneth Griffith, Angelo Muscat, Ron Grainer and many others – were all keen that we'd picked up on *The Prisoner*', explains Roger Goodman.

> The only person who thought it was appalling was Donald Sinden who said the whole thing was a load of rubbish and didn't want to be involved with it at all! Although I will say that with most of the actors we talked to – Leo McKern, Patrick Cargill, Paul Eddington and so on – there was a certain sadness that what we were asking them about was a television series and not what they considered to be their real talent, which was being able to go out and do two separate performances of a play during the same day. Even Patrick seems more proud of his early theatre roles such as *Brand* than of most of his film and television work.

In April 1979, Don Mead, an executive at ITC, called Roger Goodman with news that McGoohan was in Ireland filming a movie called *The Hard Way* with Lee Van Cleef. Immediately,

Goodman called the Dublin hotel where McGoohan was staying and got put through to his wife, Joan. After speaking with her husband, Joan called back to say that if someone could get over within twenty-four hours, he would talk. Goodman took the next plane available and recorded McGoohan's first interview for the society. Looking back over the subsequent McGoohan interviews and 'constructed texts' – and there aren't many – the interview conducted by Goodman is by far the best. McGoohan appears relaxed and, for once, happy to discuss *The Prisoner* and the themes within it. More than ten years after his series first aired, he remarked to Goodman that he still thought of himself as 'a bit of a rebel' and that he was still happiest when he was working – 'and the more intense the work, the happier I am,' he said. Talking about the last episode he revealed, 'I always knew in my mind where it had to go. I didn't have a specific ending scripted but I certainly knew the way in which it should finish and the message it should put forth. As far as I'm concerned, it works and I wouldn't change it.' McGoohan also seemed pleased that, with Six of One, there was now at least some level of positive reaction to *The Prisoner*.

'Six of One was a society waiting to happen', explains Barrie.

If I hadn't sparked it into life that December night twenty years ago, sooner or later it would have arrived. In a sense I had the easy task; the society owes everything to ITC, PolyGram, Portmeirion, *The Prisoner's* creators, the Six of

> One co-ordinators who work, for free, tirelessly into the
> night ensuring the society functions, and to the members,
> without whom there would be no society. To date, fifty
> thousand of us – all individuals, all equal.

By the end of 1978, after the last episode had been re-screened in Scotland, all ITV viewers had been given another chance to view the series, this time in colour. Similarly, in the USA, *The Prisoner* always seemed to be playing on some local, network or cable station. Despite there being only seventeen episodes, television executives weren't afraid of re-runs.

A remarkable allegory, the series left some bewildered and some completely obsessed. But it undoubtedly clicked in its time and to this day maintains a loyal band of fellow inmates engaged in discussion of the series. Thousands of people world-wide have joined the appreciation society set up by Barrie. He still writes articles, analysing episodes and, more recently, he has helped organize seminars to discuss the series' meanings. Over the years, the society has produced a wide range of impressive glossy publications under titles such as *In the Village*, *Number 6*, *Globe*, *Alert*, *Escape* and the *Tally-Ho*. The aim is to keep everyone updated on the latest *Prisoner*-related news and information as well as providing detailed analysis of particular episodes or the series as a whole. The magazines include interviews with production staff and actors as well as *Prisoner* short stories by fans keen to write about their favourite characters and themes. The unpaid Six of One volunteers also co-ordinate anniversary parties and other special events and there are Six of One branches in the USA, France, Germany and Australia. Many of the faithful followers have taken programme worship to the extreme and it's not rare for some members who live hundreds – even thousands – of miles away to travel the distance to at least one or two society get-togethers each year.

Barrie has never been worried about being labelled a prisoner of *The Prisoner*. For him, and many others, the series has been liberating:

> There are all sorts of ideas in it which encourage you to be your own person. It gives one the courage to be oneself. Each of us can escape in the sense that freedom is not about being behind bars. We make our own bars. *The Prisoner* shows us that each of us is our own prisoner and our own warder. I do think about the series every day but some people think about politics every day! If it's an obsession, it's a healthy obsession.

Although McGoohan agreed to be the Honorary President of the organization Barrie set up, he has never attended a convention. 'Six of One isn't a Patrick McGoohan fan club,' says Barrie. 'He is a very private man and his private life is kept to one side. He has invites to events but declines. The whole key of Six of One is that everyone is an individual, whether they made the series or whether they watch it.'

In the rare interviews Patrick McGoohan has ever granted, he has refused to reveal all, only ever 'explaining' a few of the symbolic aspects. Recorded on 24 and 25 of October 1982 (and aired on ITV on 12 March 1983) *Greatest Hits* looked at the year of 1968. Naturally, it examined *The Prisoner*. To everyone's surprise, Patrick McGoohan agreed to be interviewed. Although looking uneasy about the whole affair, when McGoohan spoke he remained as compelling as ever. Mike Smith asked three simple questions. But questions are a burden to others, answers a prison for oneself.

First, Smith mentioned the fact that McGoohan was more than the star of series and very much involved behind the scenes...

'I suppose I did a fair amount of things on it. I was executive producer, wrote a number of them, directed a number of them and thought it up', replied McGoohan.

'It was a confusing series to watch,' remarked Smith, 'and we all waited for the last episode, the seventeenth part, and when it got there a lot of people seemed to think they hadn't got satisfaction out of that last episode. They still didn't know who the prisoner was, why he was trapped and who was Number 1. Is there ever going to be a conclusion to that?'

McGoohan, in that familiar clipped voice, answered:

There was a conclusion – what you saw. That's why it's still confusing. They were confused and they became very incensed. In fact the switchboard at ATV was jammed

overnight and my children molested on their way home from school and people were hammering on the door with mallets at my house. We had to go and hide in Wales for a couple of weeks in the hills with no telephones or any contact with the outside world. The reason that it was confusing and that they were disappointed, I think, is because they expected the ending to be similar to a Bond thing with a mystery man, a head man, whatever they call him in Bond. It wasn't about that at all. It was about the most evil human being, human essence, and that is ourselves. It is within each of us. That is the most dangerous thing on Earth, what is within us. So therefore, that is what I made Number 1 – oneself – an image of oneself which he was trying to beat.

Finally, Smith asked him what he thought about his following: the university courses on his series and the development of the Six of One appreciation society.

'I think it's marvellous,' he replied. 'If they understand it, please pass the understanding on to me. I'd love to know what it's about!'

Other actors, however, have found it easier to express their delight at the continuing popularity of *The Prisoner*. Kenneth Griffith is one: 'I think it is one of the few optimistic signs in Britain today because this generally youthful pursuit of that strange series is a very good thing. It is about a state, our British state, and it's a prophecy as to what we are about to become, and the evidence is already very, very strong.'

Similarly, Alexis Kanner has attended a fan convention and joked it was different to how he'd expected and not full of the blue rinse brigade: 'To me, it's a bizarre experience. I was only a boy, fifteen years old at the time, so it's like someone celebrating a family event that happened in your childhood and I think it's cute. I enjoyed it at the time but I never had any idea that this would be the result.'

A few years after setting up, Six of One ran into problems. A low point was reached when members heard of a proposed plan to sell the appreciation society. Patrick McGoohan was also unhappy with certain elements of the society, seeing some actions as an invasion of his privacy. By 1981 there were various opposing factions all wanting to do their own thing and publish their own magazines and newsletters. Roger Goodman was approached by an international publisher regarding a 'professional' *Prisoner* periodical. Goodman had seen the *Dr Who* magazines on the shelves of newsagents and felt that *The Prisoner* should be up there too, nationally available to members and non-members alike. A core group of society members disagreed with his vision of the future, preferring to retain their non-profit-making 'amateur' status with its strong membership-orientated social aspect.

This bad feeling had filtered through to ITC, who subsequently ordered Six of One to suspend its activities. Eventually the company declared that Roger Langley should carry on with the running of the society. Langley had been one of the members strongly against putting Six of One up for sale, instead wanting to keep the society run as a non-profit organization:

> I began to wonder what was going on. After the end of the 'first chapter' of Six of One in 1981, I had built up the society again until there was, fortuitously, a repeat screening on Channel 4. The return of Roger Goodman to the fold, to produce a new series of *Prisoner* magazines, seemed at odds with his previous decision to end the run of *Alert* publications, on the ground that everything had been said and printed. At the annual convention I then found myself having to oppose plans to sell the society. At a subsequent convention I had an even greater fight on my hands when certain factions tried to start an opposing society. There was much bad feeling and I dread to think what would have occurred if the Internet had existed in those days. Fortunately, when I put the position rationally to ITC, it could be seen that Six of One was not trying to do anything subversive or detrimental to the series or its copyright owners and I was thankfully allowed to carry on. I never heard from the other erstwhile co-ordinator again after that time, save for a few letters threatening legal action against me.

Roger Goodman respected the decision of Six of One fans not to sell the society, but felt that he couldn't continue with what he considered an 'opportunity missed' and in August 1984 he retired from the society which he had largely co-ordinated since 1977. David Barrie left the society for a number of years but later returned as a kind of welcome figure rather than a co-ordinator (a position which he later resumed, from mid 2001). Karen Pearce (later Karen Langley) took over most of the administration and general duties. With Roger and Karen Langley at the helm, the society continued to develop, particularly from the mid-1980s. Karen Langley is now the longest-serving member and official of Six of One. She has enrolled thousands of members and deals constantly with all of the daily administration and contact with companies and advertising agencies. The Langleys have been joined over the years by various other talented *Prisoner* enthusiasts, including Larry Hall, who brought technical brilliance to the society, Bruce Clark, who was instrumental in running the society's American branch, and Arabella McIntyre Brown, who helped the society with major publicity drives. Under the new administration, membership went up significantly and at one point exceeded 3,000. It later settled at around 2,500. After the turbulent period in the early 1980s, from a base in Ipswich, the Langleys have managed to keep the society on track, retaining contact with Patrick McGoohan, dealing with ITC, PolyGram and Carlton, as well as endlessly promoting Six of One and its events.

CHAPTER EIGHT
MANY HAPPY RETURNS

'*The Prisoner* doesn't depend on any period for its meaning. You don't have to forgive it, it is not retro-kitsch, it will last for as long as people will turn their eyes to the screen and want to be entertained.'

– Stephen Fry

As well as the appreciation society, a *Prisoner* shop dedicated to the series opened in 1982 and is run from Portmeirion in North Wales, the real location of the Village and the place where fans have gathered each summer since 1977 for the annual convention. Max Hora set up the shop but 'resigned' in 1999 and left the Village. However, the shop is still open and now run by the management of Portmeirion. But for sixteen years Max *was* the prisoner:

> I liked the programme and I liked the location where it had been made. Then, after attending a couple of the conventions, it struck me that there are always people asking about the series. Before the shop, people used to ask in the café and in the shops and at the hotel. Even the gardeners and workmen used to get questions about *The Prisoner*. Where was the chessboard? What did the penny-farthing mean? Does he ever come back here? With me, I don't think it's an obsession. I've always been interested in television programmes with locations which are a bit unusual and both *The Prisoner* and Portmeirion have that individualistic touch. It's simply something I've been interested in for a long time. I suppose I made my hobby into my job and not many people can say they've done that!

Hora has even published his own series of *Prisoner* booklets focusing on the series' possible meanings, items of trivia and a whole section on the 'proper' order of episodes. For example, he believes 'Dance of the Dead' should be placed second in the series rather than eighth, because in one scene Number 6 says, 'I'm new here.' Other fans have also tried to reconstruct and reorder the series, based on quotes and dates.

A year after Hora set up his shop, in 1983, Channel 4 rescreened the series. Six of One helped the station produce an hour-long documentary to accompany the repeats. It was called *Six Into One: The Prisoner File* and included a rare interview with Patrick McGoohan.

In 1987, television cameras were back in Portmeirion, this time to film *The Laughing Prisoner*, a witty spoof of McGoohan's series by famous *Prisoner* fan, the Boogie Woogie pianist, Jools Holland. Every week, in Studio 5 of Tyne Tees Television, Holland would present the pop programme *The Tube*, but, after over a hundred shows, Jools found that something horrible was happening. He was becoming a celebrity – a prisoner of the showbiz world. His hair was becoming 'too big for his boots'. Courageously, he decided to follow in Patrick McGoohan's footsteps. In 1967, Patrick McGoohan resigned from *Danger Man*. Twenty years later, on 3 April 1987, Jools Holland resigned from *The Tube*.

'The only thing that keeps us prisoner is our own imagination… or lack of cash, or being a convicted criminal', said Jools. So, without any regard for 'Television's Upstairs', and despite an offer of fifty pounds from Roland Rivron, Jools fled the studio in Newcastle in his own Lotus 7. After handing in his resignation to the bosses of Channel 4 he returned home. By coincidence, his London home resembled that of the Prisoner – Number 1, Buckingham Place. And like Number 6 who, all those years ago, had a similar Fall Out with show business, Jools was abducted and taken to the Village.

On his arrival, he is greeted by Number 2 (Stephen Fry) who calls him Number 7. 'I am not a number, I am a television personality!' replies the new prisoner. Number 7 is then told he is one of only three prisoners left in the Village – Number 3 (Stanley Unwin), Number 6 (McGoohan, still wandering around the place) and now him.

In what is now a much quieter way of life compared to the carnival atmosphere of the 1960s Village, the only entertainment on offer is music, provided by Siouxsie and the Banshees, XTC and Magnum. However, there is a chance of freedom. The three are encouraged by Number 2 to enter a photographic competition. The lucky winner gains his freedom. Unfortunately for Jools, the winner is Number 3. Eventually, to win freedom, Jools agrees to tell Number 2 the reason for his resignation. Quite simply, it was because he 'needed a holiday'. And after a week in Portmeirion, he feels refreshed enough to return to his job as a Channel 4 pop presenter.

Returning to Channel 4, Jools thinks he may have escaped, but, as we all know, freedom is a myth and escape is a daily process. In fact, Number 7 is still working in the Television Village to this day, presenting music programmes such as *Later...* for BBC2 and *Name That Tune* for Channel 5 and he still... mixes with celebrities. Nevertheless, he does try to escape such a life as much as possible, taking to the road throughout the year with his Rhythm and Blues Orchestra.

As well as being spoofed, *The Prisoner* has often been used in the world of advertising. In September 1989, a television commercial, which cost more than three times the amount spent on one *Prisoner* episode, aired on ITV and brought Number 6 back to the screens. An advertising agency called Publicis spent £250,000 on a commercial for the Renault 21 and made *The Prisoner* trendy again. Filmed back in Portmeirion, the ad opened with a shot of the famous chessboard, filled with people dressed in *Prisoner* blazers. Cut to a Number 2 character at his console: 'Number 21 has ambitious tendencies,' he says. 'Follow him.'

Number 21 flees the chessboard and escapes the Village in... you've guessed it, a Renault 21! He then accelerates just in time to dodge Rover. 'Escape to the totally new Renault 21', says the McGoohan-esque voice-over.

The Prisoner is an obvious choice for advertising agencies who are looking to appeal to those after a touch of individuality. McGoohan's character embodies numerous sought-after qualities such as will power, strength, determination and single-mindedness.

The series has spawned a wealth of merchandise over the years, including a number of tie-in novels. These date back to 1968, when three books were published in the USA to cash in on the initial success of the series. The first, *The Prisoner*, written by the renowned sci-fi writer Thomas M. Disch, involves a mystery figure who wakes in the Village to find seventeen film canisters, each containing an episode of the series. He eventually escapes. In the second novel, *Who is Number 2?* by

David McDaniel, Number 6 is recaptured and taken back to the Village, while in Hank Stine's *A Day in the Life* the prisoner is sent on a mission to kill Number 1. These three novels, although clearly using the same basic set-up and characters, fail to capture the original's symbolic statements and deeper meaning. These novels were first published in the UK in 1979, again in 1981, and were reprinted by Boxtree in 1992.

From 1984 onwards, Six of One co-ordinator Roger Langley published his own trio of novels (*Think Tank*, *When in Rome* and *Charmed Life*) via the appreciation society. These proved far more popular with *Prisoner* fans and were reprinted many times. In *Think Tank*, a sixty-seven-year-old prisoner is taken back to the Village and put through hell all over again. Next came Dean Motter's four-part graphic novel, *Shattered Visage* (1986), which also featured the prisoner as an old man – this time alone in the Village. The novel's back cover explained Motter's premise:

It was the story of a man, who, after resigning from a top secret government agency, finds himself the prisoner of an unknown power in an ominous wonderland known only as the Village. Now, twenty years later, in an era when the mortality of covert operations is no longer taken for granted, we again find ourselves in the Village. Its fate and significance are, at last, about to be revealed.

A number of episode guides have been published over the years. One of the first was Matthew White and Jaffer Ali's

Prisoner Companion, published in 1988 by Warner Books Inc. in the USA and by Sidgwick & Jackson in the UK. This book also included quirky sections under headings such as 'Notes, Anecdotes and Nonsense' and 'What Does it All Mean?' A year later, Dave Rogers wrote *The Prisoner and Danger Man*, two books in one, published by Boxtree. This was a scene-by-scene, word-by-word account of every episode of the two McGoohan series. Around the same time, Virgin Books released *The Prisoner: A Televisionary Masterpiece* by French authors Alain Carraze and Hélène Oswald which was prefaced by an interview with Patrick McGoohan. As well as these episode guides, the series' history has also been covered in the autobiographies of those involved. Assistant editor Ian Rakoff's biography, published by B. T. Batsford, details his work on *The Prisoner* as well as his time spent on other television and film projects.

The Prisoner has also been adapted for the stage. The Post Mortem Theatre Company staged *Once Upon a Time* at the Edinburgh Festival in July 1989, while a group of Oxford University students calling themselves the Accented Images Theatre Company adapted the series for their stage version in 1994. James Goss's adaptation played at Oxford's Old Fire Station Theatre.

McGoohan's series has inspired many musicians over the years. Ed Ball came up with the track 'I Helped Patrick McGoohan Escape', while heavy metal supergroup Iron Maiden paid homage to *The Prisoner* with their release of an album called *Number of the Beast*. Another of the band's albums, *Powerslave* (1984), included the tracks *Back in the Village* and *The Prisoner*. The series' main theme tune by Ron Grainer was re-mixed in 1990 by dance producers '3 to the Power'. It was released as *The Prisoner* by F.A.B. featuring MC Number 6. The same producers also released a dance version of Edwin Astley's *Danger Man* theme. For traditionalists, the original music (including Grainer's main theme) was released on a series of albums by Silva Screen in 1989.

The Prisoner was first released on video in the early 1980s by Precision, although unfortunately episodes were edited together. Channel 5 Video then released the series in 1987 with the credits intact. Meanwhile, in the US, the series was released on video by MPI, which included the 'alternative' 'Chimes of Big Ben'. Following Channel 4's repeat screening in 1992, a box-set became available from PolyGram, who also released the American-produced documentary *The Prisoner Companion*. PolyGram also made the same video release available in Australia.

Other merchandise is constantly released and re-released, with various companies launching new *Prisoner* calendars, posters, postcards and T-shirts each year. For example, in 1997 – the thirtieth anniversary of *The Prisoner* – PolyGram aimed to make Number 6 a cool icon in the high street and launched a huge promotion campaign. A range of clothing had key phrases such as 'I am not a number, I am a free man!' emblazoned in bold lettering. Fans also got the chance to snap up a new range of mugs and key-rings, ties and bags, and an extra-cool collector's edition wrist watch. The British company

Slow Dazzle Worldwide released a calendar, Cornerstone Communi-cations launched a series of trading cards, while the series was given a re-screening on the satellite channel Bravo.

It's worth remembering, however, that original merchandise produced to coincide with the first screening in 1967 is quite rare. For example, a Dinky Toy Village Mini Moke taxi produced in 1967, discontinued by 1970, is much sought after and often attracts bids of around £200 on eBay, the Internet auction site. Like the taxis in *The Prisoner*, the Dinky model is in white with brown running boards and a red-and-white candy-striped canopy. The penny-farthing emblem appears on the bonnet, while the word 'taxi' replaces the normal number plates.

One *Prisoner* toy most fans would love to own is Number 6's Lotus 7 sports car (KAR 120C). It is now produced by Caterham Cars in Surrey, who manufacture various special editions based on the original Lotus 7, such as their 'Classic Seven' and the 'Super Sprint'. Caterham acquired the rights to produce the 7 in 1973 and, although the performance and handling have been developed over the years, the company has always retained the simplicity of the original's design. Their latest editions keep the red 1960s-look interior, alloy wheels and green-and-yellow paintwork. Graham Nearn, who was the Managing Director of Caterham Cars in the 1960s, first met McGoohan when he delivered a replacement car to the MGM studios in Borehamwood. 'Leo McKern was being lowered into a hole in the ground – out of which steam was billowing – for the final episode "Fall Out",' recalls

Nearn, now Chairman of the company. 'Viewers of *The Prisoner* will recall that in "Fall Out" Number 6's house was being prepared for his return. I played the role of the mechanic who drove up to the door of the house.'

When McGoohan agreed to endorse the limited edition Caterham Super 7, he reminisced with Nearn about the project, saying 'The Super 7 was for an individual, a free man, and it was faster than a Ferrari or Maserati.'

Patrick McGoohan was given a free replica Lotus 7 (he ordered chassis number six!) by Caterham Cars. His gift came as a thank-you for appearing at the Motor Show in Birmingham in 1990. Customers who ordered one at the NEC were invited to meet the man himself and also received a certificate of authenticity complete with a signed message from McGoohan:

> Back in 1966 when we were preparing *The Prisoner* series, we needed a car for our hero. Something out of the ordinary. A vehicle to fit his personality. The first time I saw the now-familiar Lotus Seven, KAR 120C, I had that certain feeling. It sort of looked me straight in the eye. I test drove it. This was it. A symbol of all *The Prisoner* was to represent; standing out from the crowd, quickness and agility, independence and a touch of the rebel.
>
> Many people know there were two versions of the car in the series, the second being a replica of the original Lotus Demonstrator. This replica, produced by Caterham was used in 'Fall Out', the final episode.

The 7 has been associated with *The Prisoner* ever since then and I am delighted that it remains in production today as the Caterham 7.

There have been many unofficial replicas over the years so now it's fitting that Caterham Cars should be producing an official, Limited Edition, *Prisoner* Replica. This they do with my full blessing.

I am sure you will enjoy your new acquisition. Be Seeing You. Patrick McGoohan.

McGoohan seemed in a good mood at the NEC Motor Show, even giving two interviews: one to Howard Foy of *The Box* magazine, the other to Simon Bates of Radio One. Maybe it was because news had just reached him of his Emmy win for his role as Oscar Finch in the *Columbo* episode, 'Agenda for Murder'.

With the latest release of a video and DVD box-set and recent showings on the satellite and cable channel Bravo, there have been many more new fans expressing an interest, each with his or her own interpretation.

The Prisoner's new audience, often described as 'cult', is more than just appreciative. Six of One members constantly debate the series' meanings at local meetings and annual conventions. The cult of *The Prisoner* also seems to extend to a cult of McGoohan, in which fans look for the themes of *The Prisoner* in the other (rare) appearances by McGoohan in other films and television shows. For example, they would point to the fact that in 1979 he played the Chief Prison

Warden in Don Siegel's *Escape from Alcatraz*. The fans maintain this suggests he is still thinking about the character of Number 6, presenting them with the same ideas on the individual and society. It is probably only the Six of One fans who would have noticed that in the *Columbo* episode 'Identity Crisis', for which he won an Emmy award, McGoohan plays a man who invents another personality, a dark side to his colleagues. In one scene, wearing a *Prisoner*-style jacket, he says: 'Remember the code we used in La Paz in '67, Clickerty Click.' He walks off. 'Be seeing you', he says. In another Columbo film, *Ashes to Ashes*, which aired in 1998, McGoohan plays a successful Beverly Hills funeral director, Eric Prince, who murders TV presenter Verity Chandler, played by Rue McClanahan. The final line of dialogue in the film is 'It's your funeral.' All of this may not be a coincidence when one reads a fax sent by McGoohan to the society:

```
TO ALL THE INMATES HERE PRESENT:

Why should THE PRISONER be confined twenty-five years
for having one crazy idea?  Give him a break - he has
earned some freedom and is working on his ESCAPE: See
it soon on your surveillance screens.

Nevertheless, while still incarcerated, he is most
grateful for recognition of having successfully
survived so long a sentence.

Warm regards to all concerned.


                              Patrick McGoohan.
```

This fax was read out by Roger Langley at the twenty-fifth anniversary *Prisoner* party in London in 1992. Despite his continued non-attendance, McGoohan still appears to encourage the 'recognition' of what he created. He is not the only prisoner of *The Prisoner*.

Dear Roger,

I had hoped to engineer a break at the last moment, skip over to London, unheralded, for this very special occasion and, despite my dread of such things, make an appearance.

Unfortunately there's so much going on, not the least of which is preparation of the next series, that it became impossible.

A note of gratitude, transmitted with this, had already been drafted to cover the contingency.

I can't think of anyone better than your goodself to accept the award on my behalf and I should be most grateful if you would.

Still hoping to be over in London in a few weeks, at which time we'll break bread.

Warmest regards to you and yours,

Letter and fax on previous page courtesy of Roger Langley

CHAPTER NINE
FAN CULTURE
INTERPRETING WITH THE AID OF VIDEO

'Questions of life, liberty and death are encoun-
tered in the quest to find an answer to the
simplest yet most baffling question of all: why
has the spy retired?'

– Dick Fiddy
(National Film Theatre brochure, December 1990)

'The frank non-realism of the final episode, and
of Number 6's emergence from the Village into
London, underlined the message that the Village
is, in essentials, our world at the present time.'

– Chris R. Tame
(New Libertarian Review, *September 1974)*

As an avant-garde or post-modern text, one which has served a thirty-year sentence, McGoohan's series draws on images from German expressionism, such as the films of Fritz Lang, and from the various works of Kafka and Hesse, as well as the style of French surrealists such as Jean Cocteau. The reworking of such imagery, coupled with the already strange plot, serves to provide a cultural experience in which the viewer sees many signifiers but no fixed meaning. Making meaning is what then proves to be pleasurable.

It is precisely *because* there is so much happening within the text that, despite the hostile reaction in the 1960s, the series has become an international cult over recent years. There is, of course, the international appreciation society Six of One with many members younger than the programme itself. In this section of the book, as a long-time fan of *The Prisoner*, I will present my own textual analysis of the series and of the magazines produced by other fans. This should give some insight into what exactly it is about the themes and imagery contained within the episodes that allows viewers to produce their own meanings that connect with their own social experience. Writing as a fan means I have access to the culture and traditions of this particular community, but I am also writing as a critic, based on my access to certain theories of cultural studies.

I am setting out to examine how *The Prisoner* attracts certain people to participate in the construction and circulation of shared textual meanings, sometimes going beyond the text, to activate meanings either in subordination or opposition to the dominant meanings proposed by the text. The fact that the series is allegorical where there isn't a key 'message' suggests that it allows itself to be worked on by the viewers. It invites interpretation.

The difference in audience reaction to *The Prisoner* many years after it was first screened may be seen in terms of how the series is viewed. The revelation, in 'Fall Out', that Number 1 was the evil side of Number 6 must have come as a shock to those who spotted it in the few frames it was contained in. The rest would have simply remained bewildered. In 1968, when all was revealed, once the episode had ended there was no other opportunity to go back and study the text. The initial reactions would have been fixed. However, *The Prisoner*'s new-found popularity seems to have coincided with its repeat screenings and release on video from the early 1980s onwards. Thus, further opportunities to reassess the episodes have allowed viewers to construct their own interpretations in their own time. *The Prisoner* can therefore be analysed in a similar way to the rereading of books. As one Six of One member put it: 'It's odd how *The Prisoner* both catches you and allows you freedom – in that you can't help watching the videos and reading various books and articles, but at the same time it gives you the enormous freedom to interpret it in any way, and apply it at any time.' (*Number Six* magazine, Issue 35)

One episode which has generated an enormous response from fans is 'Dance of the Dead'. In this, possibly the strangest episode of all, Number 6 finds a radio on the beach, a tool which could help him escape by telling him where exactly he is. However, after being caught with the radio he is brought to trial. In dream-like scenes Napoleon and Caesar are the judges and Little Bo-Peep the prosecutor. Sentenced to death, Number 6 then manages to escape an angry mob intent on murdering him. After running down a labyrinth of corridors he finds himself in Number 2's private chambers. A telex machine is spewing out paper. Number 6 destroys it. 'You'll never win', he says. 'How very uncomfortable for you then, old chap', replies Number 2. Finally, as if to reinforce the point, the telex machine starts working again, even though its wires have been pulled out. The prison bars slam shut once more and the viewer is left to work out what has just happened.

One fan wrote that when he first saw the episode he 'found it very frustrating: it seemed to have neither a proper story nor any clues to the mystery of Number 6's situation'. However, he confessed that after watching extra screenings of the episode he 'stopped trying to figure out the plot and just paid attention to the elements I liked most' (*In the Village*, Issue 11). Some have written in and interpreted this episode as a dream (or nightmare) of Number 6. Other fans believe that Number 6 is already dead, which would account for the bizarre sequences.

Today, *The Prisoner* is viewed from within a post-modern media culture. Video is undoubtedly a post-modern technology. Sean Cubitt believes that the success of video culture is down to the changing patterns of society, from the modernist culture of the cities to a post-modern culture of suburbia. He argues that video is beginning to dominate our cultural practices because it is 'a domestic medium, in a world in which crowds are no longer an inspiration but an object of fear: the culture of suburbia' (*Timeshift*, Routledge, 1991). The individual video viewings and readings of *The Prisoner* therefore form part of the shift from 'mass' television watching, where such series were viewed as part of a television event, to a more private style of reading. Showings of the series on certain 'specialist' television channels have certainly made it easy for it to make a lasting impression on a specific group of like-minded people. In the past decade there has been a re-run on Channel 4, re-runs on the satellite channels Bravo and Sci-Fi, another release on video and its first outing on DVD.

The VCR has also helped to bring together dedicated fans of *The Prisoner*, enabling them to watch the episodes at meetings and conventions. This allows for discussion of the series afterwards and the construction of shared meanings. As well as video, conventions at Portmeirion use the cinema in nearby Porthmadog to show episodes in the full 35mm colour format. It is the same screen where the rushes were shown after each day of filming in 1966. Until his recent sad death, even the projectionist was the usually the same person who had presented the rushes to Patrick McGoohan all those years ago. Six of One organizer Roger Langley is keen to point out the benefits of a cinema screening:

The enlargement on screen allows so many *Tally Ho* head-lines to be read, labels to be spotted on a soda siphon for example or a packet of sewing needles and badge numbers to be read. This is a delight never possible from watching videos because of the small resolution. Even with today's DVDs the definition can never match the full-screen magnification.

The *Prisoner* appreciation society Six of One has developed its role as an alternative, interpretative social community. It is a social group struggling to define its own culture and its own community in the post-modern era in which we find ourselves. Six of One is a group with a purpose. They aren't simply maladjusted social misfits but active producers, creating their own relevant meanings from the text. The group's members are not only discovering new meanings which they can share, but just by participating in this process, they are reaffirming their sense of community.

Video has changed the way the society works. Instead of simple screenings of favourite or classic McGoohan/ *Prisoner* episodes, Six of One now organizes seminars and workshops, using videotapes to expand the members' control over their series. In the seminars, some fans focus on the text's technical qualities, some on the motivation of characters and others on the analysis of the inner mean-ings. Afterwards, sets of notes are written up by those involved and are made available to the rest of the society, further adding to the idea of shared understandings. All the time, the progression of the text (through the technology of video playback and freeze-frame) is controlled by the fans themselves, something not anticipated by McGoohan thirty-odd years ago. Viewing strategies, made possible by the VCR, involve replaying important scenes at least once. This process helps create the distance needed for fans to analyse the text critically. As Cubitt points out: 'Video has enabled television to take on an emphatically Brechtian reflexivity, making transparent its recordedness, and its openness to change.'

Watching the episodes at home also allows fans to write down their analysis and send it off to the various Six of One publications. Letters in response to certain interpretations then tend to follow in subsequent issues. There are preferred meanings among *The Prisoner*'s fan community, but there is always room for other points of view. There have been various philosophical and religious interpretations of either the whole series or individual episodes.

It is no surprise that the cults of *Star Trek* and other mainstream science fiction television series are bigger than the cult of *The Prisoner*, because there are so many more episodes for fans to analyse and interpret. It is the pleasure of shared analysis to establish a shared understanding of the series which keeps most fans interested. As one Six of One member wrote:

Not only was I a member of a society of like-minded people, at long last my questions were being answered and

> in my own mind I had *The Prisoner* all figured out – well to
> my own satisfaction, anyway. Apart from just being a fan,
> I have made many new friends at the conventions who I
> keep in contact with throughout the year. Also, I have
> helped set up a local group in Leicester. (*Number Six*,
> Issue 34)

Similarly, another member wrote: 'I've resisted joining Six of One for two years (since someone lent me the *Prisoner* videos), but I'm fed up of not being able to exchange ideas with like-minded people. I think I must have confused self-imposed isolation with individualism!' (*Number Six*, Issue 35)

Also, as with other popular or cult series, fans of *The Prisoner* have tried to continue the story with their own attempts at extending the text. As well as the novels and theatre adaptations mentioned in the last chapter, each quarterly magazine produced by the appreciation society carries a short story based on the original characters. These new approaches help to expand the series' textual boundaries, constructing both histories and futures for the main characters of Number 2 and Number 6. Other fans have made their own video stories by editing together clips from existing episodes, editing dialogue and using different music.

In 1979, before and during that year's convention, a group of *Prisoner* fans made their own film, *By Public Demand*, on location in Portmeirion. It involved a female Number 2 about to retire from the Village and an election campaign to replace her. 'Same Village – Different Prisoners', read the poster's tagline. Further details were found in the publicity brochure:

> An episode-length film structured around our 1979 Portmeirion convention, which pursues the social consequences of individual 'rebellion', while taking a look at the way the Village might function today in a climate of economic austerity and advanced technology with always that human error which the Village machinery overlooks...

The film was screened at a special event at London's Institiute of Contemporary Art in September 1980 and was later released on video in 1983.

These extensions of the concept all hold on to the themes expressed in the original because, to the fans, the original series has become sacred. Talking about such 'fan art' Henry Jenkins notes that these new cultural creations help to solidify and maintain the fan community:

> What the videos articulate is what the fans have in common: their shared understandings, their mutual interests, their collective fantasies. Though made of materials derived from network television, these videos can satisfy fans' desires in ways their commercial counterparts all often fail to do, because they focus on those aspects of the narrative that the community wants to explore... (*Textual Poachers*, Routledge, 1992)

Similarly, *Prisoner* fan Edward Ball wrote and recorded the song 'I Helped Patrick McGoohan Escape', which expresses ideas of freedom shared within the programme's fan community, and draws on shared knowledge of *The Prisoner*.

In *The Practice of Everyday Life* (University of California Press, 1984), Michel de Certeau talks of textual 'poaching', whereby the viewer's own personal values are just as important as the values within the text. The reader is not passive but has a special, even playful, relationship with the text: 'Sometimes, in fact, like a hunter in the forest, he spots the written quarry, follows a trail, laughs, plays tricks, or else like a gambler, lets himself be taken in by it.' The reading de Certeau calls 'poaching' implies a borrowing of things that will prove pleasurable to the reader: 'Far from being writers... readers are travellers; they move across fields they did not write, despoiling the wealth of Egypt to enjoy it themselves.' De Certeau sees the text as 'a cultural weapon, private hunting reserve'.

The news of the possibility of a Hollywood film sequel to *The Prisoner* received a mixed reaction from defenders of the sacred text. Most fans were adamant that any film should have McGoohan's involvement, and many expressed their concern. Some talked of 'damage to the concept by a badly made film' or the way a film could 'overshadow the original enigmatic series'. One fan wrote:

Mel Gibson as Number 6? You must be joking! The end product would be a banal, straightforward affair, and

would they change *that* ending? (I hope not.) I can only urge all *Prisoner* fans to make strenuous protests. (*In the Village*, Issue 2)

Another Six of One member wrote:

It is such a sad day when we have to surrender the art that was *The Prisoner* to the blatant crudeness and commercial-ity that is Hollywood and all its ghastly trappings. I know this situation was somewhat inevitable i.e. the recent push towards nostalgia and reflection in the media and the film industry, but *The Prisoner* belongs to us – the people who have nurtured each episode... I don't think I can find the words to describe the disappointment I feel right now (all over a so-called television series). (*In the Village*, Issue 2)

It is clear from such emotional letters that part of the community's shared values regarding the series involves the understanding that, despite their respect for Patrick McGoohan, the text doesn't solely belong to him. Any 'answers' he may give in interviews are obviously valid but so too are the interpretations of any other individual who analyses or interprets it. As Six of One member Howard Foy writes: 'If he (Patrick McGoohan) didn't want people poring over *The Prisoner* – then or now – he shouldn't have made such an enigmatic series in the first place!' (*Number Six*, Issue 37). *The Prisoner* belongs to anyone who watches and appreciates it.

CHAPTER TEN
FAN CULTURE
IDENTIFYING WITH *THE PRISONER*

'Letters I've received have been fascinating. Some of them aren't at all complimentary, but the pros outweigh the cons... I had a lovely letter from a smashing feller, a colonel, you know, Order of the British Empire. "Sir," he said, "I've watched ten of them now and I've never seen such an utter load of tripe. I wish to say unreservedly that, if nothing worse happens to you, I hope the taxman gets you."'

– Patrick McGoohan, 1968

Analysis of material produced by fans of *The Prisoner* shows them to be responsive to the series' main theme of the individual's struggle for freedom in society. They are also responsive to other ideas, such as the theme of constant camera surveillance and the increasing amount of administration and bureaucracy in day-to-day life. In celebrating their text, fans are using it to rebel against these trends in society today. When they wear T-shirts emblazoned with the slogan 'I am not a number!', they aren't simply telling the world they love a particular television show; they are making a personal statement about themselves and their own attitude to life.

Devoted fans of the series often identify strongly with the lead character, Number 6, and use the ideas expressed by McGoohan in *The Prisoner* in the course of everyday life. McGoohan had something to say, and the energy of his beliefs has been picked up on by an audience sympathetic to his theme.

It is the organization of fantasy in *The Prisoner* which is so important in understanding how viewers engage with the text. It appeals to people's desires for freedom, autonomy and responsibility and allows viewers, through identification with Number 6, to imagine themselves as they would like to be. So this fantasy of individual freedom plays on wishes and desires in the lives of the television viewers. The final resolution in 'Fall Out', of Number 6 rebelling and destroying the Village, has a cathartic effect, as the resolution relates at some level to the desires of the viewer.

Valerie Walkerdine investigated the emotional effects of watching films on video in *School Girl Fictions* (Verso, 1991). In her analysis of watching *Rocky* films, she describes how easy it is for viewers to become emotionally involved with characters and events, picking up particular messages and readings: 'the film engages me as a viewer at the level of fantasy because I can insert myself into, position myself with, the desires and pain woven into its images'. She says that she identified with 'Rocky's struggle to become bourgeois'. Similarly, in *The Prisoner* viewers will identify with Number 6's oppression, because the Village acts symbolically as a prison, and suggests the idea of reacting against institutions such as the school or a place of work. From the opening episode, when Number 6 finds himself alone in the alien culture of the Village, viewers can identify with this experience of being a stranger. It is like the first day in a new job, or being a new student, or a stranger in a foreign country, and so on. Because *The Prisoner* is fantasy but is also symbolic, in that the Village could be anywhere or represent anything, there is no limit to the number of possible interpretations of the story of Number 6's incarceration. Unlike many television programmes, which provide us with an easy and unconscious way of constructing our world, *The Prisoner* is not just part of a process which contributes to the construction of our identities. Viewers can use the programme in their own ways, bringing their own social positions to the reading of the text.

Fans have written letters and articles outlining what *The*

Prisoner means to them. A fascinating finding from analysis of fans' comments is that the series has been used by many as a tool for self-analysis and for personal growth, both mentally and spiritually. They have used it to understand how they are produced and maintained as individuals in modern society. They compare their own situations with that of Number 6, who is faced with the pressure of having to conform, having his identity changed for the benefit of society. He must accept that he is a number. But Number 6 rebels and tries to hold on to his identity and individuality. He refuses to be 'pushed, filed, stamped, indexed, briefed, debriefed or numbered'. All of his escape plans fail but he keeps trying. He is a loner and sees the other Villagers as sheep-like, always obeying the authority figure, Number 2. He rarely enlists the help of others in trying to escape the Village, preferring instead to remain independent. He is successful in holding on to his identity, and he knows that he is successful. After holding his own suit up to show a maid, she asks, 'What does it mean?' 'That I'm still myself,' utters Number 6. His reply is more of a confirmation to himself that he is winning the battle with Number 1 than an explanation to the ignorant maid. The dialogue which follows, from the episode 'The Chimes of Big Ben', is also typical of Number 6's rebellion:

Number 6: Who runs this place?

Maid:　　　I don't know. I really don't know.

Number 6: Have you never wondered? Have you never tried to find out?

Later in the same episode, when he thinks he has escaped to a secret service office in London, he shouts at his superior: 'I risked my life and hers to come back here, home, because I thought it was different... it is, isn't it? Isn't it different?' Identification with this view that we should question other people and ourselves is a key factor in the viewing of the series.

The way fans talk and write about both Number 6 and McGoohan, who are two sides of the same coin, points to an extremely strong and intimate attachment to the series' creator. With McGoohan as 'Honorary President' of the Six of One society, in many ways it becomes rather like a religious cult in which fans are intensely involved with this charismatic personality. He is held in awe by most, who thank him for educating them with his ideas on the individual and society. Comments such as 'he's so charismatic that you have to pay attention to him' take up a lot of room in the fan club's letters pages in various publications.

However, they aren't all gushing. Unlike the Villagers, followers of *The Prisoner* don't blindly accept everything offered in the series. Patrick McGoohan is not their guru. The seventeen episodes as a whole seem to provide the conditions for self-analysis and personal growth, but, as a text, the programme isn't totally empowering. It is what the viewers do with the text, how it is interpreted and assimilated into their own lives, which allows empowerment. *The Prisoner* hasn't forced these people to change their attitudes and behaviour. Any change has come from within. As Six of One member David Barrie wrote: 'As Number 6 discovers, the most important relationship we have in life is with ourselves, with the part we recognize as the conscience, the inner voice, to integrate the whole. *The Prisoner* teaches us to be true to ourselves, to be an individual and to be our own guru or teacher, to be the maker of our own destiny.'

In the final episode, Number 6 is prepared to meet the beast within. *The Prisoner* teaches other people to do the same. In *Alert* magazine, member Peter Wilburg wrote:

> We each create our own personal reality... The discovery that we are responsible for what happens to us... That we are each Number 1... Today only the most courageous risk such responsibility, in thought, deed, or even... imagination. The Prisoner has such courage. He will enjoy eternal life, opening ever more doors to the Village of the self and its greater reality... That of the mind.

The idea that each individual is his own jailer, the focal point of the conclusion to the series, has been used by many of the society members who write letters about their own inner journey: 'An inner struggle with oneself has to happen as well as the outer struggle – sort yourself out before you start trying to sort out the world, or you just make a mess of things...' (Pantha Waterworth, *Number Six*); 'It is fear that makes us all prisoners of ourselves' (Peter Tiahnybida, *Alert*).

Another society member, M. Kyriacou, confessed to using *The Prisoner* as a route to freedom. Previously, he had been doing the 'sensible thing', but after viewing the series he decided, 'that's it – I'm going to do what *I* want, and reach my own goal... Thank you, Six of One... for teaching me to fulfil my desires, and not the desires of the majority.' Es Why, also a member, wrote of his journey of self-discovery:

> How this unique series has contributed to my spiritual growth... a journey of wonder and magic... ultimately liberating... truth is not absolute... We cannot tell the truth to another, for it may not be their truth... The prison we have to escape from is ultimately created by ourselves. Each of us, and each of us alone, holds the key. It's an irony of life that the more we understand our imprisonment, the freer we can become... Many thanks Patrick McGoohan.

Thus, *The Prisoner* enables a form of self-help to take place. Using the lead character as a role model, viewers interpret the action from the standpoint of Number 6 throughout the series, as if they are in his shoes. This process is extended beyond the programme when the viewers play out their own real lives from his vantage point. Number 6 is the ultimate hero who never gives up. Viewers can compare their own behaviour with his. Number 6 has clear principles and, unlike the mass of conforming Villlagers, he values himself. Viewers can use the character of Number 6 to analyse their own strengths and weaknesses. R. Price looked at the way we use heroes in an article in *Saturday Review* (USA,

December 1978): 'As we scan their dazzling faces and feel their strong pull [we] scan ourselves – probe our weaknesses and know which of them need filling and why.'

In psychological terms, a related point is that in writing down certain statements about their own identity, even before sending them off to the society magazines, Six of One members have made clear statements to themselves. Also, the fact that Number 6 is successful in holding on to his identity helps to validate the fans' role-modelling actions. Snow *et al* noted similar effects in their study of American students who watched the series as part of a university degree course in the 1970s.

Glancing over the letters pages of the Six of One publications reveals that there are just as many women identifying with Number 6, even though he is a male lead character. This is because, although male, the character is presented within the allegory as asexual. McGoohan avoids sexuality throughout the series. In a 1976 interview for *Danger Man* magazine, he said: 'I abhor violence and cheap sex... we need moral heroes. Every real hero since Jesus Christ has been moral.' The desexualized nature of Village life can be seen in the episode 'Dance of the Dead', in which a carnival dance lacks any real emotion and is completely sexless. McGoohan wanted Number 6 to be the opposite of sexist characters like James Bond, the lucrative role he turned down twice. In fact, according to Alexis Kanner, McGoohan turned down millions of dollars offered to him just to talk with producers about playing 007.

Number 6 is an Everyman figure who can be identified with by both sexes. The same can be said for Patrick McGoohan himself. Through a short-lived television series, a large group of people have been transformed by his vision of what can be achieved by an individual in society. He has shown how it is possible to be oneself. Just as Number 6 made choices to reject Village life, McGoohan has also rejected what most other stars crave for. He shuns publicity and hardly ever gives interviews. Perhaps this adds to his magnetism. People want what they can't have. *Prisoner* fans can only have McGoohan as Number 6 (or in other film and television roles) but they can't seem to get very close to the man behind the thing that has changed their lives. Most fans have accepted that they should respect McGoohan's privacy. Those who haven't have tended to regret their actions. One Six of One member wrote of how he planned to meet McGoohan at the British premiere of the film *Braveheart*, and of the consequences:

> It took me a few heart-pounding seconds to grasp the enormity of the wonderful situation I now found myself in! Mr McGoohan was very casually dressed in a sports jacket, collar and tie, and slacks. And no one took any notice of him. No one, except me. Eagerly I shouted a welcome to him and that I had a gift for him... Our eyes met, I waved the package at him, and he flinched... I was suddenly ashamed of myself and my behaviour and I was distressed at his distress. (*In the Village*, Issue 10)

This fan goes on to ask whether the Six of One society should continue after McGoohan's distress. However, the fact that this fan decided to confess to what happened, rather than forget the incident, reveals how fan culture operates. The above letter elicited a huge response in the next issue, which included letters from fans who also felt the appreciation society might have been suffocating McGoohan. However, most of the letters had a similar tone. The majority agreed that any contact with their Honorary President should be 'pre-arranged' and fans should respect his decision as to whether he wants to meet them or not.

This all indicates that as well as there being shared understandings within the fan culture of the text in question, there are also shared understandings or guidelines as to how the fan subculture should be guided in relation to that particular text and its stars.

Although made in the 1960s, *The Prisoner* has a certain timelessness about it, mainly due to the fact that it deals with ideas and themes which are still relevant today. The battle to remain oneself in a society increasingly obsessed with conformity to mass consumerism strikes even more of a chord today. Fans of *The Prisoner* have shown themselves to be responsive to McGoohan's message to reject this way of life and the world of superficiality and image. Their identification with these ideas in the series is what has led them to become fanatical, adapting *The Prisoner* to their own lives. McGoohan's portrayal of individualism has allowed for the comparison with their own situations. Fans too are prisoners of their own lives, financial situations and families. *The Prisoner* doesn't let them think that they can be completely free in society. Fans know this isn't possible. What the series does assert is that we can strive to be as free as possible within our situation, rather than simply sitting back and not questioning anything.

Contrary to the negative stereotypes of fans as controlled, passive and abnormal, the many followers of *The Prisoner* aren't simply consumers but are proactive in many ways. Using the ideas in the series, they have constructed their own identities. *The Prisoner* has therefore been a source of strength for fans using the self-empowerment their fandom gives them to take control of the meanings of their own lives, enabling them to perform more powerfully in their social world. As a post-modern text, *The Prisoner* allows the possibility of shifting subjectivities on the part of the viewer in that he or she can choose whether or not the idea of a rational, coherent self can exist or not. It is possible to accept that Number 6 is presented as the ultimate in-control individual or that he is suffering from a complete identity crisis because of the society in which he lives. *The Prisoner*, as an open text, allows viewers to participate in the creation of meaning and, although viewers may be identifying with yet another television hero – McGoohan/Number 6 – because he is seen as an ideal person to emulate, they are involved in making their own specific readings. Because it provokes a wide range of possible meanings, *The Prisoner* allows its viewers the pleasure of understanding it in relation to their own subcultural meanings and pleasures, and at the same time adds to their own understanding of the social system and their social experience, and thus in turn their own subjectivity. Part of the viewers' pleasure will derive from the fact that they know the meanings they have made are not necessarily those intended by the original writers and producers. In resisting a simple interpretation of *The Prisoner*, on the entertainment/adventure level, viewers who have, for example, identified with the series on a spiritual level, or who have used it as a tool for self-analysis, will find pleasure in having exercised the power to do this.

Fans have extended this source of private pleasure, through meetings, conventions, fanzines and so on, to create their own subculture in which the pleasure becomes a social experience. The technology of video has been the major force in helping fans to analyse the series, either individually or together. Repeated viewing through the use of VCRs has helped people develop and redevelop complex theories relating to the series. Attracted by the individualism expressed in *The Prisoner*, they have formed their own sub-culture/village/society. Enjoyment is to be had through sharing *The Prisoner* with each other and this shared philosophical outlook has become a major part of many fans' lives. However, they maintain their autonomy through the diversity of their natures, backgrounds and locations. The appreciation society acts as a meeting place of like minds and allows them to revel in fan culture. These individuals come together as a social group only when they agree to do so.

CHAPTER ELEVEN
UPDATING THE PRISONER

Many fans have always hoped for a *Prisoner* remake or update. The idea was first mooted by Lehlan Rogers (brother of Kenny) in the early 1980s. He had planned to make a futuristic version, replacing the Village with the City, but nothing ever came of it. Then, from 1993 onwards, other rumours began circulating. Some stories even suggested that Steven Spielberg was interested in buying the rights.

In 1995, PolyGram Television International acquired ITC Entertainment and executives (including Lord Grade) confirmed that a movie version of *The Prisoner* was still on the cards. On 13 December 1998, the one man who could have helped pull it all together quickly, Lew Grade, died of heart failure at the London Clinic. Shortly after, Carlton Communications acquired the ITC film library for $150 million. With over 5,000 hours of television, Carlton found itself in a prime position to allow re-runs of shows like *The Prisoner* on its own cable and digital channels in the UK. Also, since Carlton was one of the largest DVD manufacturers in Britain, *The Prisoner* was seen as an obvious choice for release in this new format. It was therefore no surprise when episodes were quickly re-mastered for this new format and released with lots of added extras and special features.

In 1999, five years after rumours first emerged of a Hollywood remake of *The Prisoner*, the film production rights for ITC shows (separate from television screening rights) were acquired from Seagram by USA Films, headed by former Paramount/Twentieth Century Fox boss, Barry

Diller. The deal involved Propaganda Films – already linked with the *Prisoner* movie.

Simon West, director of *Con Air* and *The General's Daughter* was thought to be keen to make the new *Prisoner* film, funded by Propaganda, with a script not by McGoohan but by Larry Konner and Mark Rosenthal. It was hoped the USA Films/Carlton deals would end all of the uncertainty regarding the *Prisoner* film.

Indeed, by the end of 1999, a movie of *The Prisoner* was in the development stage. At the time, Simon West was astounded by fans' knowledge of his plans:

> I don't know how they manage it but they have so much information about what we're doing. I look at the Internet and everything we are doing is there. I was mesmerized. They have so much information. There's obviously a mole somewhere because they know every little detail about decisions we're making. It's amazing – like something out of *The Prisoner!* But it's good because it gets the buzz going.

By September 2000, a new name was attached to West's project. Rather than Konner and Rosenthal, a different writer was working on a script for the *Prisoner* remake. Christopher McQuarrie (*The Usual Suspects*) was quoted as saying he would remain true to the original concept and that he would do 'everything possible not to contemporize it… The characters work the way they were. I'm going to go straight up, old school.' Hollywood producer Barry Mendel (*Sixth Sense*) was also on board and the trio (West, McQuarrie and Mendel) were all opting to return to the original source material rather than McGoohan's new screenplay, that he had written at the time of filming *Braveheart* in the early 1990s and hoped Mel Gibson would both direct and star in.

News of a film remake by West was seen as a result both of his love of the original series and also of the popularity of big-budget Hollywood films which ditched big bangs and car chases. Most notably, the success of *The Truman Show* in 1998 seemed to help offset the disappointment of the tatty film version of *The Avengers* (an all-time stinker) and help speed up the development of a *Prisoner* production.

The Truman Show was a surprise hit because it dealt with quite complex and dark *Prisoner*-esque themes of the loss of personal freedom and identity. Based on a script by Andrew Niccol, who also wrote the sci-fi cautionary tale *Gattaca*, this deceptively light-hearted film was directed by Peter Weir (*The Cars that Ate Paris/Witness/Green Card*) and starred Jim Carrey as Truman Burbank.

The Prisoner explored the idea of constant surveillance by having Number 2 and the Supervisor watching Number 6's every move from the Control Room in the Village. *The Truman Show* is in some ways an updating of that idea. The idyllic coastal town of Seahaven, where Truman Burbank lives, is reminiscent of the Village. It is a huge sound-stage constructed inside a dome – 'one of only two man-made structures visible from space – the other being the Great Wall of China,' according to the TV producers who adopted

Truman at birth and took over every aspect of his life without his consent.

Seahaven is in fact a real Florida town called Seaside rather than a Hollywood set. Weir decided on this real-life location because of its similarities with the ideas he had for the fictional Seahaven. Seaside is a planned community of 300 cottages with its own self-contained shops. Individual in style, it was designed by Robert and Daryl Davis in 1980 in a similar manner to Clough Williams-Ellis's development of Portmeirion. Residents of Seaside have to adhere to strict rules concerning the maintenance of the cottages.

In Seahaven, 5,000 secret cameras are broadcasting every detail of Truman's life, including intimate conversations with his wife and family – who are really actors – to millions around the world. Truman is the victim of a global confidence trick. His life is the most extraordinary reality show in the world.

The Truman Show is already almost a reality: one girl in America carries a camera around with her all day, every day, webcasting her entire life on the Internet, and then there are television shows such as *The Real World*, *Cops* and *Jerry Springer*. In Weir's film, 'The Truman Show' is shown twenty-four hours a day and is the most popular TV show in the world. Truman is the world's biggest television star and he doesn't know it. Weir wanted to go even further into the idea of the television hoax and couple it with real technological advancements. He had proposed having every theatre that showed the film equipped with video cameras to take shots of audience members and project them into the actual movie. This would have reinforced the idea that the 'real life' audience watching Weir's film is very close to the audience watching 'The Truman Show'.

Weir's film is a very odd escape story. It is smart and funny – set in a parody of the superficial suburban American world of cheery greetings, blue skies and picket fences. But after thirty years of living in this artificial biosphere, Truman begins to realize that all is not quite right. His quest for the truth – and, ultimately, freedom – begins.

Ed Harris is as authoritative as ever. He is Christof, the creator and producer of the ongoing broadcast, a real Number 2-type character watching from his control centre, suspended high above Seahaven disguised as the moon. He controls Truman's world not only through the script, which is followed by all of the paid actors posing as family and friends, but he also controls the weather – for example the setting of the sun. He can talk directly to the 'co-stars' via hidden earphones and can therefore cope if Truman's suspicions are aroused by having 'extras' on hand to divert his attention.

Harris has a commanding on-screen presence and is cast perfectly in this role, having already shown a similar kind of ferociousness in Alex Cox's bold political satire *Walker*. Interestingly, Dennis Hopper was originally cast as Christof, but he left the set early on in the project in what is said to have been a mutually acceptable agreement between him and Weir.

In *The Truman Show*, as in *The Prisoner*, the viewer becomes part of the escape story, willing the hero to overcome all oppression and fight for freedom. When Truman realizes he is in a completely fake world and attempts to break free, the viewer roots for him, but at the same time identifies with his situation. A deliberate effect of the film is for a kind of questioning to take place – the questioning of what is real and what is constructed, and the idea that we should begin to test the boundaries of our own universe.

Although similarities with *The Prisoner* are numerous, when questioned about the series, Weir says, 'I did look at *The Prisoner* but I didn't find it much help. The big difference being the [television] audience is complicit with what's going on in *The Truman Show*. I think probably the single film that occurred to me was *Dr. Strangelove*. In terms of tone – humour mixed with major drama – Kubrick pulled it off. He walked the line!'

Paramount must have had a lot of tough decisions to make regarding the promotion of the film. In the end, they opted to market it as a comedy. The promos didn't draw attention to the themes or to the dramatic side of the film. Although this simplified the piece somewhat, it also helped to attract cinema-goers who might not usually have opted to watch something as dark and unusual. Similarly, Vincenzo Natali's *Cube* (1998) was another surprise hit. This interesting low-budget escape story posed plenty of questions but answered few. A group of strangers who wake up in a mysterious maze-like prison have no idea how they got there and have to fight for their freedom.

Hollywood often caters for the lowest common denominator of everything but, like their precursor *The Prisoner*, films like *Cube* and The *Truman Show* are proof that the discussion of fate and free will *can* be expressed in mainstream entertainment.

However, *The Truman Show* ends with the hero actually earning his freedom. As in another piece of Hollywood Kafka, *Groundhog Day*, there *is* a happy ending. Perhaps it would have been more telling if Truman had not been able to escape the artificial world of Seahaven, but at least the ideas are there, even if they aren't pushed as far as they might have been.

In the summer of 1998, *The Truman Show* was the movie of the moment. London's West End was filled with posters saying 'Free Truman Burbank'. The success of *The Truman Show* sparked a huge amount of industry buzz over the possibility of a *Prisoner* remake. Rumours ranged from Mel Gibson being approached by Patrick McGoohan to Steven Speilberg desperately trying to get the rights. A few showbiz reporters asked whether a woman could play Number 6 – Cate Blanchette? Julia Roberts? The casting remains to be seen – as, of course, does the film.

CHAPTER TWELVE
BACK BEHIND BARS
KINGS, ALCATRAZ AND OTHER
MEMORABLE MOMENTS

'Of the four of us who got out, Angelo's gone,
Patrick lives in seclusion in Pacific Palisades, Leo
lives in seclusion in Bath and I'm in seclusion in
London. We're a diminishing group of escapees.'

– Alexis Kanner (The Kid/Number 48)

A number of colourful figures were introduced in the course of *The Prisoner*, but it was the final two episodes which brought the four most colourful together. They were, of course, Patrick McGoohan, Leo McKern, Alexis Kanner and Angelo Muscat – all of whom supposedly escaped from the Village. Of the four actors, Muscat is the only one who has died: 'It was really sad when Angelo passed away,' says Kanner. 'He was such a warm, gentle person, one of the kindest people I've met.'

After *The Prisoner* had been made and after witnessing the general hostility towards the programme's complex conclusion, McGoohan escaped to Switzerland before moving permanently to California, where he has lived since the controversy, distancing himself from continued speculation and revealing nothing. He has a reputation for being a reclusive actor, rarely giving interviews, and he is very particular about the films he chooses to appear in. In fact, he was offered the part of James Bond *before* Sean Connery and again when Connery quit the role, but turned it down each time because it wasn't the type of role he wished to play. He also turned down the role of *The Saint* because he didn't like the car, a Volvo, which was to be used in the series.

Kanner now resides in London, although he spends a lot of time in Los Angeles and is in regular contact with McGoohan: 'Pat is the only guy I know who can call me long distance, about three and a half thousand miles away, talk, hang up and then turn up on my doorstep completely unexpectedly on the same day. He's a man of many moods and has a very flexible relationship with space and time!'

Now in his eighty-second year, Leo McKern, like McGoohan, no longer talks about the series. In fact, he has talked less about it than McGoohan. Both actors were under tremendous strain during the production, with masses of dialogue to remember, as nothing was improvised. Kanner has also revealed an added worry for McGoohan: 'After the show, Pat was exhausted. Then he had a really big shock. His daughter went through a life-threatening illness which everyone said was incurable. She was apparently going to be either a quadriplegic or dead and so he devoted five years to becoming an expert in this and he cured her.'

After *The Prisoner*, Patrick McGoohan took on various roles in the 1970s and hardly any in the 1980s. Some of the more notable productions he has appeared in seem to be similar in nature to *The Prisoner*, dealing with the same themes, which suggests that the concept is still as important to him as ever.

For example, ten years after *The Prisoner* was made, in 1977, Alexis Kanner took McGoohan hostage for his directorial debut, *Kings and Desperate Men*. The former *Prisoner* Kid wrote the lead role for him, that of John Kingsley, a radio talk-show host who is held hostage in his penthouse broadcasting studio by a history teacher-turned-terrorist leader called Lucas Miller (played by Kanner) and forced to host a strange trial over the airwaves.

Kanner had the idea for the plot during a family visit to

Montreal at the time of the Olympic Games. A chance meeting with the head of security led to the theme of a terrorist take-over. Everyone was worried that the massacre of Munich was about to be repeated and the detective in charge had to prevent such an occurrence:

> While I was sitting opposite him, I noticed, upside down, a private bulletin that had been issued to ten or twelve of the metropolitan police chiefs of the largest cities of North America, and it was headed 'Anticipate random killings in the Eighties and Nineties'. Of course, he wouldn't let me see the contents but it was the word 'random' which really got to me – random, out of the blue, some guy steps out of a crowd and shoots the President, the guy who lived next door to you all your life climbs up a flagpole with an automatic weapon and starts shooting students on a university campus. It was that idea of random terrorism, combined with the narrative of a failed Shakespearean actor becoming a great AM commentator on some North American radio station. That's Patrick – he is the King in *Kings and Desperate Men*.

Most of the film's main scenes were shot in December 1977, with some re-shoots in 1978. It premiered at the Montreal Film Festival in 1981 and was released in Canada and the UK in 1984, although it wasn't until 1988 that *Kings* found a distributor in the States.

The film begins with fragmented images of the gang of

terrorists on their way to hijack Kingsley's radio show. These muddled pictures are coupled with an extraordinary array of voices, phones, loudspeakers, sirens, gun blasts and other strange noises and dialogue. This is all intercut with Kingsley interviewing a judge who has just passed a fifteen-year sentence on a man convicted of hitting and killing a policeman while driving a car. Miller and his followers believe there has been a gross miscarriage of justice and so take over the live show and let the people decide. Another group of Miller's gang hold Kingsley's wife and young son in their down-town apartment.

Back in 1967, McGoohan had been so impressed with Alexis Kanner's performance in 'Fall Out' that he showed his appreciation by having his name 'boxed' in the closing title sequence. Ten years after being directed by McGoohan, the roles are reversed, with Kanner in the director's chair: 'Actors are very vulnerable when they work, especially when they are out on a very long limb, playing a tremendously difficult part', says Kanner.

Patrick's part in *Kings and Desperate Men* required a tremendous commitment and trust from him, so he didn't have any of his producing, writing or directing hats on. He was very much dependent on what the guy standing next to the camera would tell him at the end of each take and before the next take. The role reversal never occurred to either of us but I suppose he must have listened to me as I listened to him all of those years ago doing *The Prisoner* –

though I never threatened him with a day of 'indescribable brutality'!

'There wasn't another English actor in my mind who could conceivably have risen to the heights that he did in that performance. I was thinking that if Patrick really was unavailable for it, I would have to rewrite the whole thing and make the character an American comic played by someone like Johnny Carson, and have him as a broken-down clown comedian. But the character, as written and conceived, could not have been played by any other actor.

This film particularly merits attention because, like *The Prisoner*, it is ablaze with intelligence and thought-provoking themes. Billed as 'the Englishman's Englishman, the man you love to hate', Kingsley begins his radio show with a quote from John Donne: 'Thou art slave to fate, chance, kings and desperate men.' Later, the two men sing lines from 'God Rest You Merry, Gentlemen', even though one is holding a gun and distorting people's lives. So, on one level, *Kings and Desperate Men* becomes a modern morality play: 'It's a spiritual odyssey,' explains Kanner. 'Miller and Kingsley have had this date a long time. They're ready for it. Kingsley was always going to meet himself the other way one day. It was a date with destiny.'

Described by critics as 'mesmerizing' (*LA Times*), 'fascinating to watch and every bit as compelling to listen to' (*Hollywood Reporter*) and 'innovative and compulsive' (*Time Out*), *Kings* is a brilliant tour-de-force which reunites two electrifying performers. F. X. Feeney of *LA Weekly* wrote: 'This is a remarkable film, one of the very best. Suspenseful, stylistically daring, wonderfully acted, its strengths are many – the photography and editing, the performances nothing short of splendid – it's wonderful to watch.'

Many critics have said that *Kings and Desperate Men* sees McGoohan's finest performance in a film role. 'Patrick was thrilled with the picture,' admits Kanner. 'I saw one article in the press in which Patrick actually said he could die happy, now that his grandchildren could see an example of what he was capable of in *Kings and Desperate Men*. We were both delighted with the end result. Of course, now Patrick is playing in *Braveheart* and *The Phantom* and *A Time to Kill* and suddenly it's a new lease of life!'

In fact, the press reaction to *Kings and Desperate Men* was good across the whole spectrum of the media, something which surprised the director:

The thing that I found most remarkable about the media response, particularly here in Britain, was that it was the high street as well as the cinema buffs and it was the glossy magazines as well as tabloid newspapers. I had never anticipated that it would cross like that because I had gone out of my way not to make *Die Hard*, which they later made. I had gone out of my way to make a kind of psychological thriller about some very serious subjects. There are of course some parallels with *The Prisoner* – issues about power and coercion and the ethics of who holds the gun. In fact,

who controls the skyscraper is the same kind of question
as who controls the Village. But that's eternal.

A few years after the release of his film, Alexis Kanner was
asked to remake *Kings and Desperate Men* with another actor
in Patrick's place. He turned down the offer instantly: 'A
major studio – never mind which – wanted it remade with
an American actor because they thought that the situation
was really neat. I said no but later it was done anyway.'
Indeed, many film critics noted the similarities between
Alexis Kanner's film and the Bruce Willis action flick *Die
Hard*. The theme was the same – a tense hostage situation on
the thirtieth floor of a city skyscraper on Christmas Eve.
Even the dialogue that Alan Rickman speaks in *Die Hard*,
playing Kanner's part, has distinct similarities. 'Now everybody's doing the hostage movie,' laughs Kanner. 'It's a
really big franchise. In *Independence Day*, they take the
whole Earth hostage!'

Following the release of *Die Hard*, a list of similarities
was drawn up by the producers of *Kings and Desperate Men*.
It became the lead story on *Entertainment Tonight* and was on
the way to the Ninth Circuit Court of Appeal when Kanner
decided life was too short. He'd been caught up in endless
litigation at the expense of doing what he enjoyed most –
acting and directing.

In 1979, McGoohan was back behind bars, this time co-
starring with Clint Eastwood in one of the best prison films
ever made – *Escape from Alcatraz*. Based on the novel by

J. Campbell Bruce, with a screenplay by Richard Tuggle, the film was directed by Don Siegel and had Eastwood as the prisoner, a cunning bank robber called Frank Morris. McGoohan is equally powerful as the psychotic control freak of a warden. Number 6 becomes Number 2! One critic, Harry Sheehan, has pointed to the startling clarity of Siegel's central themes – 'the conception of character and the moral acceptability of antisocial or violent behaviour to preserve that character against the oppression of a conformity-crazed society'.

Escape from Alcatraz is a moody suspense thriller, a bleak and downbeat tale based on fact: an account of four convicts' escape plan and eventual breakout from the Rock, the infamous maximum security prison at Alcatraz. As in *The Prisoner*, escape seems impossible: 'We don't make good citizens but we do make good prisoners,' says McGoohan's character, who takes great delight in making orders and removing prisoners' privileges. One inmate, Chester 'Doc' Dalton (Roberts Blossom), is devastated when his beloved painting privileges are taken away, after the warden sees a rather unflattering portrait of himself. 'No reform is possible for Alcatraz,' remarked Henry Sheehan, 'because it is not the prisoners who are psychotic, but the warden. Played by Patrick McGoohan with that actor's fondness for personal psychosis, the head warden is a tight-lipped control freak with a habit of instituting gratuitously repressive rules. He is utterly out of his mind and completely in charge.'

'Alcatraz was built to keep all the rotten eggs in one

basket,' snaps McGoohan's warden. 'I was specially chosen to make sure that the stink from the basket doesn't escape. Since I've been warden, a few people have tried to escape, most of them have been recaptured. Those who haven't have either been killed or drowned in the bay. No one has ever escaped from Alcatraz and no one ever will.'

On 13 June 1962, however, Frank Morris and two other inmates broke out. They had all made papier mâché dummy heads to fool prison guards into thinking they were fast asleep when they were actually digging their way out with spoons. Using a raft made of driftwood and raincoats, they all disappeared into the cold waters of San Francisco bay and were never seen or heard of again. The film's ending is slightly optimistic with McGoohan finding a chrysanthemum, the flower associated with Doc's paintings, on nearby Angel Island. But the fact that these habitual criminals were never heard of again suggests it is more likely their escape attempt failed and they didn't make it to the mainland.

This film, like *The Prisoner*, seems to have achieved cult status, having been chosen to be part of BBC 2's Moviedrome season in 1992. The presenter of this cult movie strand, British film director Alex Cox (*Repo Man/Sid and Nancy*) – who also kindly wrote the foreword for this book – made it quite obvious that he was a big fan of *The Prisoner*. Cox, who had at one point expressed interest in directing a film remake of the series, turned his introduction to *Escape from Alcatraz* into a salute to McGoohan and the series:

Since we've already exhausted the standard reference works and databases, to say nothing of your gentle ears, with information about Siegel and Eastwood, I propose instead to talk about the second featured player of this almost all-male cast, Patrick McGoohan.

McGoohan was the star of a very popular TV series in the early Sixties – *Danger Man*, apparently called *Secret Agent* in the States. McGoohan followed this with a remarkable series of his own devising, *The Prisoner*. There are some, myself included, who believe that it was the greatest TV series of all time. You've probably seen an episode or two on one of the commercial channels. Actually, you probably know exactly what I'm talking about.

The Prisoner was a bizarre, apocalyptic, Cold War Kafka nightmare in which McGoohan awoke in a bizarre prison colony (Portmeirion in North Wales) to face endless interrogations from a series of absolute leaders all named Number 2. McGoohan's character's name, of course, was Number 6. Number 6 denied he was a number and insisted he was a free man. But every week when he tried to escape he'd be betrayed or sprayed with hallucinogenic drugs or smothered by a gigantic floating beach-ball and brought back to the holiday camp. McGoohan directed several episodes, including I believe its incomprehensible but brilliant two-part finale, which apparently had to be improvised when the second series was terminated at short notice. It was a brilliant piece of television, which as yet has not been made into a film. How about it, Patrick?

The Prisoner is now a cult of the first order. You can buy books about it, even attend Prisoner conventions. McGoohan went on to direct a feature musical based on Othello, titled Catch My Soul. Rather like one of the weirder episodes of The Prisoner called 'Living in Harmony', Catch My Soul was set in a desert commune. Variety called McGoohan's direction 'taut', but the Monthly Film Bulletin said the film was 'arguably even less watchable than the unspeakable Godspell'.

After that, McGoohan appeared in various movies, including a weirdly compelling spaghetti Western produced by Sergio Leone called Un Genio, Due Compari e Un Pollo, and Baby, the film about the baby dinosaur. In Escape from Alcatraz, ten years or more after he played Number 6, he plays another character without a name – the warden of the impregnable high-security jail on Alcatraz Island. Interesting: Number 6 has become Number 2. Clint Eastwood is Number 6...

Alex Cox has since thanked McGoohan for what he described as 'your great contribution to the expansion of my mind when I was but a wee nipper and as an artist ever since'.

Is it really just a coincidence that after playing a prison guard in Arthur Dreifuss's The Quare Fellow in 1962 – a film version of Brendan Behan's play which shows the agony of prison life – McGoohan chose to play a prisoner in The Prisoner and later on a power-mad warden in Escape from Alcatraz?

Another notable appearance by McGoohan was in David Cronenberg's 1981 picture *Scanners* where he plays Dr Paul Ruth, an evil man who manipulates science for his own good. Scanners are people who can manipulate and explode other human beings, using only the power of their own minds. One scanner, called Revok (Michael Ironside), plans to use his talent to control the world. McGoohan's character, however, finds a scanner who is as powerful – Cameron Vale, played by Stephen Lack – whose mission becomes the attempt to infiltrate Revok's faction. Dr Ruth always seems to be trying to advance the human condition although this still has horrific repercussions, such as the exploding of someone's head in an early scene. McGoohan is quite at home in a film about the destructive potential of the human mind – and in the mysterious setting that Cronenberg creates. During filming, McGoohan explained: 'David has a special style that appeals to me. It's been a long time since I've enjoyed an acting experience so fully. Our minds seem to mesh. We both like the unusual, the slightly mystical and mysterious.'

McGoohan has had parts in some made-for-TV movies such as *Of Pure Blood*, *Jamaica Inn* and *Three Sovereigns for Sarah* and he continues to have guest roles in Peter Falk's *Columbo* series. In 1991 he won an Emmy award for his role as Oscar Finch in *Columbo*: 'Agenda for Murder', an episode he also directed.

However, his role as King Edward I in *Braveheart* in 1995 saw the welcome return of McGoohan to the big screen after a ten-year absence, his previous major motion picture having been Walt Disney's *Baby – Secret of the Lost Legend*, released in 1985. *Braveheart* was a film full of excitement, emotion and spirit and another story concerning a desperate fight for freedom. McGoohan's role as King Edward was one he played with both quiet rage and frustration. It was followed up with a role as a judge opposite Donald Sutherland in the film version of John Grisham's courtroom drama *A Time to Kill* in 1997. In the same year, McGoohan starred as the eccentric Dr Harvey Langston in Rene Daalder's psychological, science fiction thriller *Hysteria*. 'I run a lunatic asylum, so there is absolutely no acting required,' he joked during an interview for the movie's publicity notes. The character is a complete reversal of Number 6. Here McGoohan is playing a man bent on using the power of 'the group mind' rather than the power of the individual: 'When minds have learned to mingle. When no thought is wholly one's own. When one has had too much of the other ever to be himself alone. Then only do we know what it is to be human,' explains Dr Langston. 'Man has failed to create a working society since he walked out of the soup. Wouldn't it be wonderful, even at this late hour, to have a true universal consciousness. Think about it – every moment, of every day, someone, somewhere is falling in love. If only we could tap into that we would all be fools in love forever.'

There's no doubt that McGoohan's performances are often memorably nerve-racking. His tremendous presence is suggestive of a psyche on the brink of explosion due to untold pressures. Patrick McGoohan is an actor who seems to prefer playing roles of men in isolation, apart from the mainstream of society. He clearly identifies with loners who are as enigmatic as he is. The characters he has played are men who have rejected the rules, refused to play the game and lived their own way. These roles may provide the clearest insight into the very private mind of one extremely fine man – a man who has had the will and the strength to follow his own individuality.

APPENDICES

APPENDIX I

PATRICK MCGOOHAN – A DETAILED LISTING OF HIS WORK

1948–1957

As well as various roles in plays at the Sheffield Repertory Theatre in his early years, McGoohan appeared on some of the most prestigious stages in London's West End during the early 1950s. Shortly after appearing in *Serious Charge* at the Garrick, he played opposite Orson Welles in *Moby Dick* at the Duke of York's Theatre. A year later both McGoohan and wife Joan played in *Ring for Catty* at the Lyric Theatre. However, it was Ibsen's *Brand* which won him critical acclaim.

In these early years McGoohan had supporting roles in the following films:

1954: *Passage Home*
1955: *The Dam Busters*
I Am a Camera
The Warriors
1957: *Zarak*

1957–1960

Lead roles in films for McGoohan began when he became a contract player for the Rank Organisation. *High Tide at Noon* (1957) was the first of four. *Hell Drivers* (1958) saw

McGoohan as Red, a trouble-making trucker, in this sturdy drama directed by Cy Endfield, which also co-stars David McCallum, with a very young Sean Connery in one of his early bit parts. *The Gypsy and the Gentleman* (1958) is a wildly theatrical costume drama which sees McGoohan as Melina Mercouri's love interest. *Nor the Moon by Night* (1958) was the last film with McGoohan under contract with Rank. These films brought him great recognition and parts in TV plays such as *The Greatest Man in the World* (1958), *Brand* (1959) and *The Big Knife* (1959), which led to…

1960–1966 The *Danger Man* Years

On the strength of those live TV plays, Lew Grade picked McGoohan to play John Drake, the NATO special security agent in *Danger Man*. The series was known as *Secret Agent* in America. There were three main seasons – the first, with thirty-nine thirty-minute episodes, was made in 1960–61 and was the forerunner of the numerous spy series and films which followed. After the first season, McGoohan returned to his film career for a while:

1961:   *All Night Long* – McGoohan as a jazz drummer in an updating of *Othello*.

   Two Living, One Dead – McGoohan stars in this tense drama as a bank teller who is criticized for his actions during a robbery. This film is brilliantly directed by Anthony Asquith.

1962:   *Walk in the Shadow* – An intelligent film directed by Basil Dearden which has McGoohan as a doctor

caught up in a battle between the individual's right
to express religious beliefs against the rights
of society.

The Quare Fellow – McGoohan in a setting that is to
become very familiar – a prison! He plays a guard
who changes his mind about capital punishment.

Two films followed for Walt Disney – *The Three Lives of
Thomasina* and *Dr Syn, Alias the Scarecrow* – both in 1963,
before *Danger Man* resumed production in 1964. This second
season saw a few changes. Now, McGoohan's character John
Drake was a secret agent for England rather than for NATO
and the thirty-two episodes were extended to hour-long
stories to allow greater insight into the mind of an individual character. The third season began in 1965 and the final
season in 1966 only lasted two episodes (in colour) which
were combined to make the film *Koroshi*.

1966–1969

After tiring of the role of John Drake, McGoohan approached
Lew Grade about *The Prisoner*. It was made by McGoohan's
production company Everyman Films in 1966 and shown in
1967. Of the seventeen episodes, McGoohan starred as
Number 6 in each of them and was also credited as executive
producer on all of them. He wrote and directed 'Free For
All', directed 'A Change of Mind' and 'Many Happy
Returns' and also wrote and directed the final two episodes,
'Once Upon a Time' and 'Fall Out'.

During a break in the filming of *The Prisoner* McGoohan travelled to America to play another British secret agent opposite Rock Hudson in *Ice Station Zebra* (1967) directed by John Sturges.

1970–2002

After moving to Switzerland and then California, McGoohan continued with his film career: *The Moonshine War* (1970), *Mary, Queen of Scots* (1971) and *Catch My Soul* (1974), in which McGoohan tried out the *Othello* theme once more, this time as director rather than as the star.

In 1974, he began what was to become a lasting relationship with America's favourite crumpled TV detective, Columbo. He worked with Peter Falk on three episodes of the 1970s series, which are so well produced that they stand up as individual films rather than episodes of a television series. McGoohan's performance in *Columbo:* 'By Dawn's Early Light' (1974) won him an Emmy award for Outstanding Single Performance by a Supporting Actor in a Comedy or Drama Series. The following year he was back with Falk in 'Identity Crisis', another *Columbo*; this time though McGoohan directed as well as guest-starred in a film filled with allusions to *The Prisoner*. Many called this the eighteenth episode of *The Prisoner*, what with McGoohan being dressed in a very *Prisoner*-esque jacket and from time to time greeting people with the familiar 'Be Seeing You'. His final stint on *Columbo* in the 1970s was as director of 'Last Salute to the Commodore' (1976).

APPENDIX I

In 1975, McGoohan appeared in, but didn't seem too involved in, *The Genius*, a farcical Italian spaghetti Western. In fact McGoohan has gone on record as saying he hasn't even seen this film. He was back working for Lew Grade's ITC in 1976 in a TV movie of Alexandre Dumas' *The Man in the Iron Mask*. In the following year he was back as another bad guy in the highly rated comedy-thriller *Silver Streak*, a film which saw the first pairing of Gene Wilder and Richard Pryor. 1977 saw the short-lived American TV series *Rafferty* (thirteen episodes) followed by the reunion of McGoohan with Alexis Kanner in what is, arguably, McGoohan's finest performance in a film – as the talk radio host John Kingsley in the critically acclaimed *Kings and Desperate Men*, although this film wasn't released in Britain until 1984. After the MGM classic *Brass Target* (1978), 1979 brought the release of another great prison film, *Escape from Alcatraz* (1979) with McGoohan in the role of the warden. Also in 1979 he went back home to Ireland to film *The Hard Way*, which was followed by the filming in Canada of the Cronenberg sci-fi/horror classic *Scanners*.

A few TV movies followed: *Trespasses* (1983), *Jamaica Inn* (1985) and *Three Sovereigns for Sarah* (1985), and then what could have been another Disney classic, *Baby – Secret of the Lost Legend* (1985). It was a good idea to have McGoohan as a mad palaeontologist, desperate to take credit for discovering dinosaurs in the African jungle but, in the end, the cast were let down by an appalling script.

Later in 1985 the acclaimed play *Pack of Lies* marked his

return to the stage for the first time in ywenty-five years and it was his first Broadway performance.

The TV movie *Of Pure Blood* (1986) and a guest role in *Murder She Wrote* (1987) saw out the 1980s for McGoohan, but in 1991 he was back directing and guest-starring in another *Columbo* episode with Peter Falk. Once again he was rewarded for a superb performance in 'Agenda for Murder', one of the best *Columbo* films. He came to England in 1992 to film the drama *The Best of Friends*, in which he played George Bernard Shaw, for BBC TV.

In 1995 McGoohan played King Edward I in *Braveheart*, the top film of that year. In 1996 he played the gentle judge in the tense courtroom drama *A Time to Kill*. He also played the supporting role of the father in *The Phantom* and co-starred in the film *Hysteria* in the same year.

Then, in 1998, McGoohan directed and guest-starred in another *Columbo* film for ABC in the United States called 'Ashes to Ashes'. He was also credited as co-executive producer. And more recently he wrote and directed the *Columbo* teleplay 'Murder with Too Many Notes'.

Finally, McGoohan's latest project has been his role as executive producer in the development for *Con Air* director, Simon West, of a planned new film version of *The Prisoner*.

APPENDIX II

THE PRISONER –
STORY INFORMATION
FROM AN ITC/ATV PRESS BOOK, 1967

T.V. SERIES – WORKING TITLE – 'THE PRISONER'

1. Our hero is a man who held a highly confidential job of the most secret nature. He therefore has knowledge which is invaluable or highly dangerous depending which side of the fence he falls.
2. He resigns.
3. He is 'computerized' to the 'retired' file.
4. He is abducted from his home and transported unconscious to a place.
5. Is he abducted by 'Us' or 'Them'?
6. He awakens in a village.
7. He discovers that the village is a self-contained unit of our society with its own Council of Parliament.
8. He is treated with dangerous courtesy and invited to participate in all village activity.
9. He can stand for election on the Village Council and is invited to do so.
10. He is given a cottage with maid service and every conceivable modern amenity.

But:–

1. Every inch is bugged. His every move is watched on closed circuit television.
2. He has to have a Security Number to warrant an issue of village currency to enable him to buy food supplies, clothing, or even a glass of beer in the village pub.
3. In his cottage is a detailed map of the village with all exits clearly marked but they are cut off by a deadly ray barrier.
4. Some of the residents encourage him to try and escape. Others attempt to dissuade him.
5. They are all known by numbers, and he cannot distinguish between a possible ally and a potential enemy.
6. Who are the Prisoners?
7. Who are the Captors?
8. All persons at all times behave with excessive normality against a background of sinister abnormality.
9. They all speak English. Sometimes a foreign language is heard in distant conversation but ceases on his approach.
10. There are no out-going telephone calls.
11. The Village Post Office returns all mail and cables – 'Unknown'.
12. Who then runs the village?
13. Is it 'West' training him up to top indoctrination resistance?
14. 'West' infiltrated by 'East' trying to break him?
15. In any event – he is a prisoner.

THE ACTION IS ON THREE LEVELS

1. Our hero constantly probes to discover why he is a prisoner and who are his captors.
2. He strives by all means and at risk of death to escape.
3. He becomes involved with his captors and takes an active part in situations arising in their lives.

BACKGROUND

1. The prison is a holiday-type village.
2. GEOGRAPHY

   The village lies on a peninsula and covers five acres. It is completely isolated by a range of mountains that cut it off from the outside on the north-west and by dense forests on the north-east. For the rest it is surrounded by sea

   A flat beach, a mile long is a prominent feature of the village.

   There are cliffs and caves and two old mines go deep in the bowels of the earth under the village.

   The communal life of the village gravitates round thirteen main 'blocks' of buildings, villas, bungalows, shops etc.
3. COMMUNICATIONS

   Telephone lines to the outside world are not available. There is no bus service, no railway station, taxis do not go outside the village. There is a closed circuit T.V. service.

4. NAME

The village has no name. It is just the village or 'here' or 'this place'.

5. TRANSPORT

The village has a taxi service of mini mokes with girl drivers. There are flying strip facilities (on the beach or lawns) for helicopters to take off or land.

6. SHOPPING

The village has a tiny number of shops. The most important is the General Store which supplies everything.

7. CURRENCY

The village uses its own. There are Units which are issued in lieu of any known currency. There is also a Credit Card system.

8. THE INMATES

There are two kinds – those who have been taken there and those who run it. But we cannot necessarily tell who is who.

9. INDUSTRY

There is no one single industry in the village, but the people are kept busy doing all kinds of work. There is a factory manufacturing local requisites.

10. HOSPITAL

There is a hospital which is also in actual fact a conditioning centre using the latest methods. It is situated in the Castle which stands in a clearing by itself.

11. SURVEILLANCE

Constant. Television cameras record every move and

activity both indoors and outside. Every type of modern electronic surveillance system is used to keep tabs on everyone.

12. AMUSEMENTS

All catered for. There are entertainment facilities of all kinds, from chess, dancing, gambling, film shows. There is a Palace of Fun to keep 'em happy. And amateur theatricals.

13. DEATH

The village has its own graveyard.

14. KEY BUILDINGS

These include:

1. The Labour Exchange which assigns people varied tasks, 'drafts' them to wherever they are wanted, organizes and runs the inmates.

2. The Citizen's Advice Bureau. Here all the inmates' problems can be solved.

3. The Town Hall. The municipal office and headquarters of the chairman.

4. The Palace of Fun.

5. The Hospital.

6. The open air café.

15. NEWSPAPER

The village produces its own.

16. T.V. – RADIO

The village has its own units being particularly concerned with local news.

APPENDIX III

The following article was written by a journalist who attended the 1967 press conference. Anthony Davis also managed to gain individual access to McGoohan.

PATRICK MCGOOHAN TALKS...
BY ANTHONY DAVIS

It ends this week... the nightmarish cat-and-mouse game of spirit-sapping tortures, subtle, scientific brainwashing and malignant mind-probing...

All the will-bending, talk-inducing techniques employed against the luckless Number 6. All his abortive escape bids and rather more successful table-turning techniques.

The last episode of *The Prisoner*, the most bizarre thriller series ever, is at hand. The moment when viewers will expect the answers to the questions they have been asking since this intriguing, two-level blend of special agentry and science fiction began sixteen curious episodes ago.

This is Patrick McGoohan's series. He devised it, was executive producer and starred in it. He had a hand in writing every script and directed a number of its episodes. Never before has one man been so responsible for a series, let alone such a remarkable series.

Before it began he said: 'If people don't like it, there's only one person to blame – me!'

Well, people have liked it. They have also been confused, baffled, bewildered and irritated by it; by its gimmicky switching of characters playing the oppressive Number 2; by its secret symbols like the old bicycle and the mute midget butler; by its timeless gadgetry and strange, convoluted plots.

I sought McGoohan's end-of-term views on the series. His aides shook their heads. Pat had not talked to a journalist since the series started on the screen, they said. He had been working day and night, they said. He was no seeker after personal publicity, they said. He preferred to leave the public to pronounce on his work, they said.

But the unpredictable Pat declared that he would talk to me about the series.

Now, I have seen Pat relaxed, talkative and charming. I have heard how brusque and crushing he can be when a newspaperman attempts to probe his more private thoughts. When I talked to him he was supervising the cutting of this week's final episode of *The Prisoner*. And he acted like Number 6 at bay, fighting to preserve his secrets from a new Number 2.

He volunteered nothing, answered laconically, or with two questions for the one asked. It was a magnificent, exasperating performance.

What, I asked him, were his feelings as his series came to an end?

He shrugged that off. 'I've done a job,' he said, crisply.

'I set out to make a specific number of films. I've made them. The series has come to an end. It's just the end of a job, that's all.'

Had he achieved all he hoped to achieve when he embarked on the project?

'It was meant to be controversial and it has been', he said. Pressed further, he added: 'If it has failed in some respects it's a pity, but I don't think it has. Letters I've received have been fascinating. Some of them aren't at all complimentary but the pros outweigh the cons. Eleven million people watched it every week. What more do you want?'

Was stirring controversy his main aim?

'Who said so?' Pat demanded. 'Are you saying that? Oh, you're asking. The series was posing the question, "Has one the right to tell a man what to think, how to behave, to coerce others? Has one the right to be an individual?" I wanted to make them ask questions, argue and think. I like to provoke argument at all times. I'm provoking it now.'

Thus provoked, I told him the thing that bothered me most about *The Prisoner* was the absence of any continuity between the episodes; that there was no logical progression in his captors' extraordinary attempts to break him, no logical pattern to his escape bids or, indeed, to anything else.

He snapped back, 'Let me ask you two questions. You're living in this world? You must answer "yes" to that,' he went on hopefully, without a pause. 'Do you find it always logical? No? That's your answer to that.'

I said some people had found the obsession with medical experiments on Number 6 verged on the sick or sadistic. He was back fast again. 'A man died after a heart operation. You read about that? How about that operation? Do you find that sick or sadistic?'

And so the conversation went on, mainly question for question.

I asked at what stage he decided on the ending? This brought a clear answer. 'I envisaged it from the beginning. In a series like this, you have to know at the outset what you're aiming at. You have to know the ending before you can begin. So I had the idea for the final episode first of all and took it from there.'

And would the final episode answer all the riddles?

'What riddles?' he demanded.

'The riddle of what country the village is situated in, who runs it, and who is Number 1?' I asked.

'No,' he said. Pushed further: 'No; it doesn't.'

A programme company spokesman was more informative: 'The answers are there in fact, but not in black and white, not answered straightforwardly at surface level. The viewer will still have to use some imagination and read between the lines.'

I can add a little to that. I have seen a synopsis of the final episode titled 'Fall Out'. It's written by Pat. Directed by Pat. Starring Pat. And I can tell you that most of it is set in an underground cavern beneath the village, where Number 6 is on trial.

With Pat's permission I can tell you that Number 6 is confronting a former Number 2 (played by Leo McKern), whom viewers saw meet his death in an earlier episode.

But with the devious-minded McGoohan in charge, there is much more below the surface than appears.

Footnote: Pat was firm on one point. Will *The Prisoner* ever return in another series? 'Definitely not', he said.

Original article by Anthony Davis, published in 1968. Reproduced by kind permission of *TV Times*.

APPENDIX IV

SCRIPT PAGES

Reproduced courtesy of Carlton International Media Limited

CALL SHEET   SECOND UNIT

PRODUCTION: ..THE..PRISONER.............................

EPISODE :...........".FREE FOR ALL"........................

DATE: .Thursday,..15th..September.
7.30 a.m. leave
UNIT CALL :.....8.00..a.m...on..set....

DIRECTOR : ..........DON..CHAFFEY.........

SET/Sc. No's.   (1) COVER ALL TAKE-OFFS, LANDINGS & MID-AIR(HELICOPTER) WHILST
FIRST UNIT IS SHOOTING.
(2) PREPARE SPEEDBOAT TO COVER Scs.94,97,100,104,106,108,110,
112,98pt, DAY.

ARTISTE	CHARACTER	D/R	MAKE-UP	ON SET
PATRICK McGOOHAN	PRISONER		When available from 1st Unit	
DOUBLE A.N. OTHER	FOR MR. McGOOHAN		8.00	8.30

PROP. VEHICLES.   2 Mini-Mokes to run taxi service for Hotel Patrons.
1 Mini-Moke with 2nd Unit, and 1 with 2nd Camera Crew.

PROPS. Lifejackets, Water Skis, background dressing for Old People's Home.

PROD.   2 Dowty jet speedboats and Camera Boat to be on set at 8.00 a.m.
Protective clothing for Camera Crew and Director.
Ground to air radios.
Helicopter from 1st Unit.

WARDROBE. Towels.   Double for 'P's clothes.   Bath robes.

ART/CON.   Punt to be rigged for sea to shore landing.
Hides for parked cars required.
General village dressing required.

CATERING. As per 1st Unit Call Sheet.

TRANSPORT. Members of the Unit must not bring their cars into the hotel
grounds during the time that the helicopter is here.

TERRY LENS
FIRST ASSISTANT

*Photographs of helicopter and pilot, Charles James, reproduced for Six Of One
by kind courtesy and copyright of ITC Entertainment*   - Overleaf

41

EXT.   COUNTRY LANE.   DAY. LOC.   161

PANNING THE TRUCK THROUGH. THE CHORUS OF "DEM
BONES" GROWS IN VOLUME. DIMINISHES AND FADES
OUT ALTOGETHER AS THE TRUCK DISAPPEARS INTO
THE FAR DISTANCE.

EXT.   M.1.   DAY.   LOC.   162

SHOOTING FROM BEHIND A BOWLER-HATTED DRIVER
AND ALONG THE GLEAMING BONNET OF HIS ROLLS-
ROYCE MAKING GOOD HEADWAY PAST A SIGN READING
"LONDON" - 28 MILES". HE ADJUSTS HIS RADIO.
A DELICATE PIECE OF MOZART HARDLY LOUD ENOUGH
TO DISTURB THE TICKING OF THE CLOCK. THE
HIGHWAY STRETCHES BEFORE HIM.

HE IS APPROACHING AND ABOUT TO OVERTAKE A
TRUCK. HE FROWNS AND ADJUSTS THE RADIO AGAIN.
THE MOZART IS BEING DROWNED OUT BY A LUSTY
RENDERING OF 'DEM BONES". HE PULLS OUT TO
OVERTAKE THE TRUCK.

"DEM BONES" IS NOW AT CONSIDERABLE VOLUME.
HE SWITCHES OFF THE RADIO IN EXASPERATION AND
AND LOOKS OUT HIS LEFT HAND WINDOW. HE IS
LEVEL WITH THE TRUCK. HIS JAW DROPS. HE SEES:

EXT.   THE TRUCK. DAY. LOC.   163

THE BARRED SIDE OF THE "CAGE". WITHIN P, NO.2
AND THE YOUNG MAN IN FULL VOICE. P IS MOVING
FROM THE COOKER WITH A POT OF STEAMING COFFEE
WHICH HE SERVES TO THE OTHER TWO. THEY WAVE
CHEERILY AS THE ROLLS GOES BY.

INT.   THE ROLLS. DAY. LOC.   164

IT PASSES THE "CAGE". BRINGS THE CABIN OF THE
TRUCK INTO VIEW. THERE IS NO DRIVER IN SIGHT.
THE STEERING WHEEL APPEARS TO MOVE OF ITS
OWN VOLITION.

EXT.   M.1. DAY. LOC.   165

THE ROLLS ACCELERATING AT ENORMOUS SPEED
AWAY FROM THE TRUCK TOWARDS LONDON.

INT.   TRUCK CABIN. DAY. LOC.   166

THE BUTLER DRIVING. NODDING HAPPILY IN
TIME TO THE MUSIC. HE CANNOT BE SEEN ABOVE
THE DOOR BUT HAS SUFFICIENT HEIGHT FOR THE
WINDSCREEN.

42

.EXT. M.1. DAY. LOC. _____ 167

THE TRUCK APPROACHING IF THE DISTANCE. "DEM
BONES" GROWING IN VOLUME. IT SLOWS AND
PULLS INTO A LAY-BY. THE SONG FADES.

EXT. LAY-BY. DAY. LOC. _____ 168

TRUCK COMING TO A HALT. THE YOUNG MAN DESCENDS
FIRST. FOLLOWED BY P AND NO. 2. THEY SHAKE HANDS.
THE YOUNG MAN MOVES TO THE CABIN OF THE TRUCK
AND RAISES HIS HAT TO THE BUTLER WHO BOWS.

                        YOUNG MAN
              Got to keep moving, man,

HE TURNS AND CROSSES THE ROAD. STARTS WALKING
BACK. THUMBS A LIFT OF PASSING CARS. P AND
NO. 2 WATCH HIM A MOMENT THEN ENTER THE "CAGE".
THE TRUCK IS UNDER WAY AGAIN AND PULLS OUT.

EXT. M.1. DAY. LOC. _____ 169

P AND NO. 2 WAVE TO THE YOUNG MAN THROUGH
THE BARS OF THE "CAGE". HE REMOVES HIS HAT AND
HOISTS IT IN SALUTE. HE DIMINISHES INTO THE
DISTANCE, WALKING.

                                  CUT TO:

C.S. OF LONDON POLICEMAN. DAY. LOC. _____ 170

HE TURNS IN A COMPLETE CIRCLE SLIGHTLY
PERTURBED. "DEM BONES" SEEMS TO BE WORRYING
HIM. ZOOM BACK AND WE SEE WHAT IS ON HIS MIND.

EXT. TRAFALGAR SQUARE. DAY. LOC. _____ 171

THE POLICEMAN STANDS CENTRE OF THE SQUARE.
CIRCLING IT - THE TRUCK. FROM THE "CAGE"
- "DEM BONES". THE TRUCK LEAVES THE
SQUARE AND HEADS DOWN WHITEHALL.

EXT. WHITEHALL. DAY. LOC. _____ 172

THE TRUCK PASSING THROUGH.

EXT. HOUSE OF LORDS. DAY. LOC. _____ 173

THE TRUCK PULLING INTO THE NEAREST PARKING
METERS ADJACENT TO THE HOUSE OF LORDS.
IT STOPS.

APPENDIX V

CONTACTS

Six of One – *The Prisoner* Appreciation Society
The group publishes *Free For All*, a quarterly magazine of an extremely high standard, and also acts as a constant source of information regarding issues relating to the series. They can be contacted at their base in Ipswich – PO Box 66, Ipswich IP2 9TZ, England. Please enclose a stamped, self-addressed envelope for a reply. If overseas, send two International Reply coupons.

***The Prisoner* shop and information centre**
It can be contacted via the Portmeirion Village Hotel, Penrhyndeudraeth, Gwynedd LL48 6ER, Wales, or by visiting the shop itself which is open throughout the year. There was an official opening ceremony on 11 June 1999, presided over by the Welsh Parliamentary representative and the resort's Managing Director, Robin Llywelyn (grandson of Clough Williams-Ellis).

The Prisoner is available on Carlton video and DVD. The original music from the series is still available on the Silva Screen record label. Other merchandise is available through both the appreciation society and the shop.

APPENDIX V

INTERNET SITES

At the time of writing this book there appears to be a growing number of websites dedicated to the discussion of *The
Prisoner* on the Internet. Six of One organizer Roger Langley
has recently commented on the amazing growth in *Prisoner*
websites:

> There are some sites which contain nothing but links to other
> *Prisoner* sites and it is now possible to go upon a *Prisoner* jour-
> ney or odyssey through cyberspace which could last a whole
> month before one might return to the original starting point.
> Photographs from the series are held on servers around the
> world and no doubt one day somebody will store every
> single piece of information and image and soundbite from
> *The Prisoner* in one enormous living and breathing website!
> There have even been websites dedicated to Patrick
> McGoohan which have brought about a sharp response from
> the actor, causing these to close down. There is possibly no
> equal amongst actors with regard to his ability to bring
> about fearful compliance if he barks a command.

Here is a selection of *Prisoner* websites:

www.ThePrisonerAppreciationSociety.com

The official Six of One website promoting the appreciation
society with details of how to sign up for the packed quarterly
mailings and special offers plus links to all the latest *Prisoner*
news. There's also a link to the Six of One convention page.

www.sixofone.org.uk
Another official Six of One site.

www.portmericon.com
Six of One's convention site.

www.stevenpauldavies.com
The author's official site with full details of his other film
and television books.

www.portmeirion.wales.com
and **www.portmeirion-village.com**
The official Portmeirion page, a history of the Village and
its creator Sir Clough Williams-Ellis – a guide run by the
Portmeirion staff and the *Prisoner* online shop.

www.hometown.aol.com/theprsnr/index.html
On this site you can download *Prisoner* theme music, the Iron
Maiden *Prisoner* track, as well as vote for your favourite
episode. This page also doubles as a site for another strange
series which borrows heavily from *The Prisoner* – *Nowhere Man*.

www.geocities.com/Area51/4031
A site which includes some amazing original artwork and
graphic montages inspired by the series.

www.the-prisoner-6.freeserve.co.uk
This offers an extensive range of information, graphics, orig-

inal artwork and music as well as information and graphics on *Danger Man*. A midi-enabled wavetable 16-bit sound card is essential for playing the music files.

www.retroweb.com

A great site by Kipp Teague with a wealth of information, images and a few rarities. There's an episode guide, a picture gallery, trivia page and a 'what's it all about' section. Other television shows looked at in detail include *Star Trek* and *Northern Exposure*.

www.avalondreamtime.co.uk/dman.htm

A complete dossier of *Danger Man* – a world of 'guns, girls, gangsters and glamour!' There are key dates, an episode guide, cast and crew information, trivia pages as well as picture galleries and a John Drake classic quotes section.

BIBLIOGRAPHY

Ali, J. and White, M. – *The Official Prisoner Companion*. London: Sidgwick & Jackson, 1988.

Berger, P. – *Invitation to Sociology*. London: Penguin, 1963.

Carraze, A. and Oswald, H. – *The Prisoner: A Televisionary Masterpiece*. London: Virgin, 1990.

Cubitt, S. – *Timeshift*. London: Routledge, 1991.

Curran, J., Morley, D. and Walkerdine, V. (eds.) – *Postmodernism: The Rough Guide*. London: Arnold, 1996.

Donald, J. – *Sentimental Education*. London: Verso, 1992.

Eco, U. – *The Role of the Reader: Explorations in the Semiotics of Texts*. Bloomington: Indiana University Press, 1979.

Fiske, J. – *Understanding Television*. London: Methuen, 1987.

Fiske, J. – *Television Culture*. London: Methuen, 1987.

Foucault, M. – *Discipline and Punish*. London: Penguin, 1979.

Giddens, A. – *The Constitution of Society*. London: Polity Press, 1984.

Gregory, C. – *Be Seeing You*. Luton: John Libbey Media, 1997.

Huxley, A. – *Brave New World*. London: Chatto & Windus, 1932.

Jenkins, H. – *Textual Poachers: television fans and participatory culture*. London: Routledge, 1992.

Langley, R – *The Prisoner in Portmeirion*. Portmeirion Ltd, 1999.

BIBLIOGRAPHY

Lewis, L. – *Adoring Audience: Fan culture and popular media.*
London: Routledge, 1992.

Lodge, D. – *Working with Structuralism.* London: Routledge,
1981.

Mead, G. H. – *Mind, Self and Society.* University of Chicago
Press, 1934.

Orwell, G. – *Nineteen Eighty-Four.* London: Secker &
Warburg, 1949.

Postman, N. – *Amusing Ourselves to Death.* London:
Heinemann, 1986.

Price, N. – 'The Heroes of Our Times' in *Saturday Review.*
USA, December 1978.

Rogers, D. – *The Prisoner and Danger Man.* London: Boxtree,
1989.

Rose, N. – *Governing the Soul.* London: Routledge, 1990.

Snow, R. et al – 'Learning and Self-Counseling Through
Television Entertainment' in *Teaching Sociology*, Vol. 7,
No 1. USA: Sage Publications, 1979.

Walkerdine, V. – *School Girl Fictions.* London: Verso, 1991.

ABOUT THE AUTHOR

After graduating from Goldsmiths' College, University of London, Steven Paul Davies joined Virgin Radio, becoming the youngest ever news presenter on national radio in the UK. He is the author of *Alex Cox: Film anarchist* and *A-Z Cult Films and Filmmakers* and the co-author of *Brat Pack: Confidential*. Steven is currently writing for *The Guardian* as well as working on his new book, *Get Carter and Beyond: The cinema of Mike Hodges*. He is based in Hereford and London.

www.stevenpauldavies.com

INDEX